LYNNE PICKERING

ART AND INTERIORS

PORTRAITS

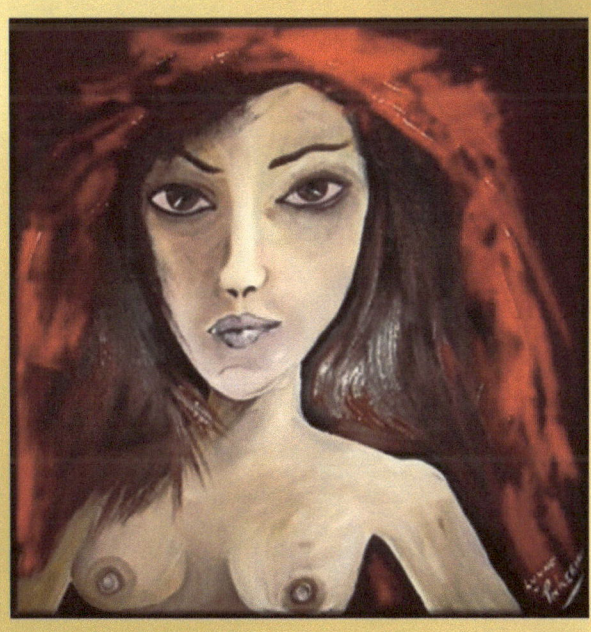

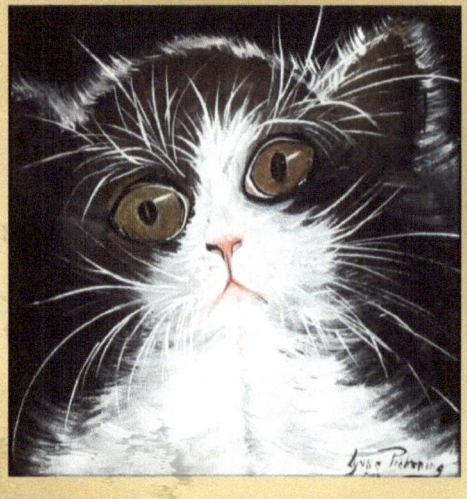

DEDICATION

To my loving husband who without the patience to pack my art so carefully I would have not
Sold over 5,500 paintings in over 32 countries.

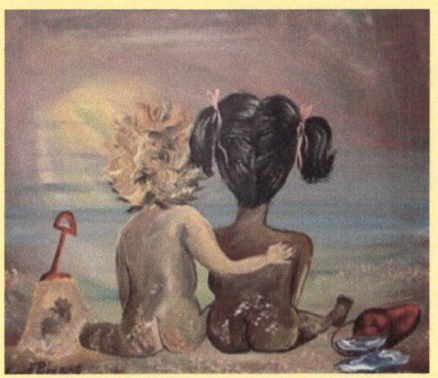

Some of these paintings have been a finalist in art shows.
The Bald Archy
2008 Nicole Kidman   : The Devil wears Prada in Urban Country, toured Australia for 10 months
2007 Peter Costello. Treasurer Forever ; wearing Budgie Smugglers. Toured Australia for 10 months
There are notable portraits of Supreme Court Judges Paintings held in Chambers
A Painting for the Archibald Prize MP Laurence Springboard.
And many finalist paintings.

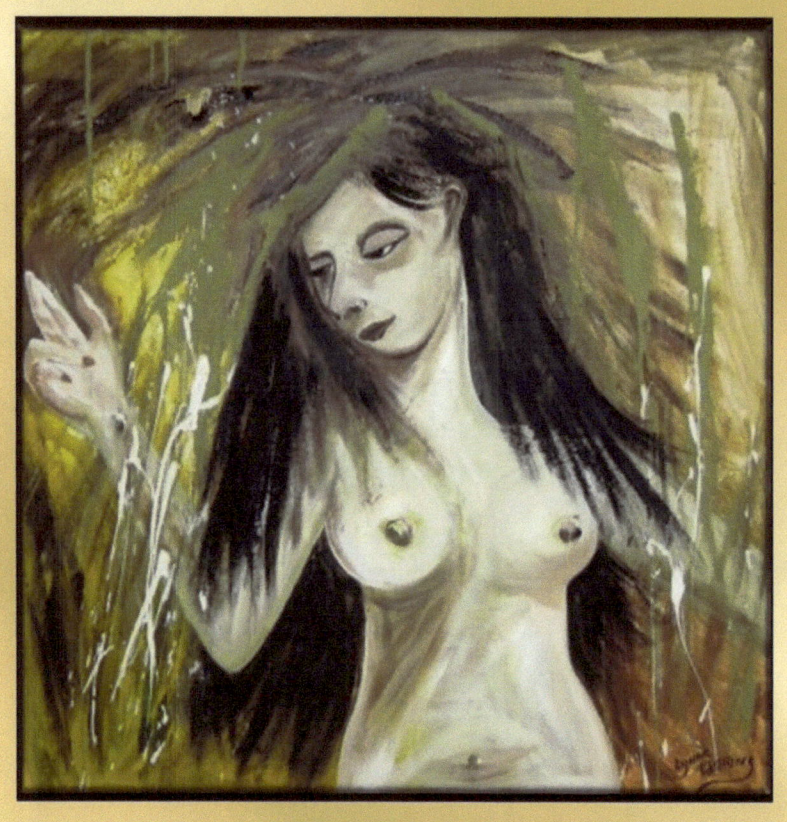

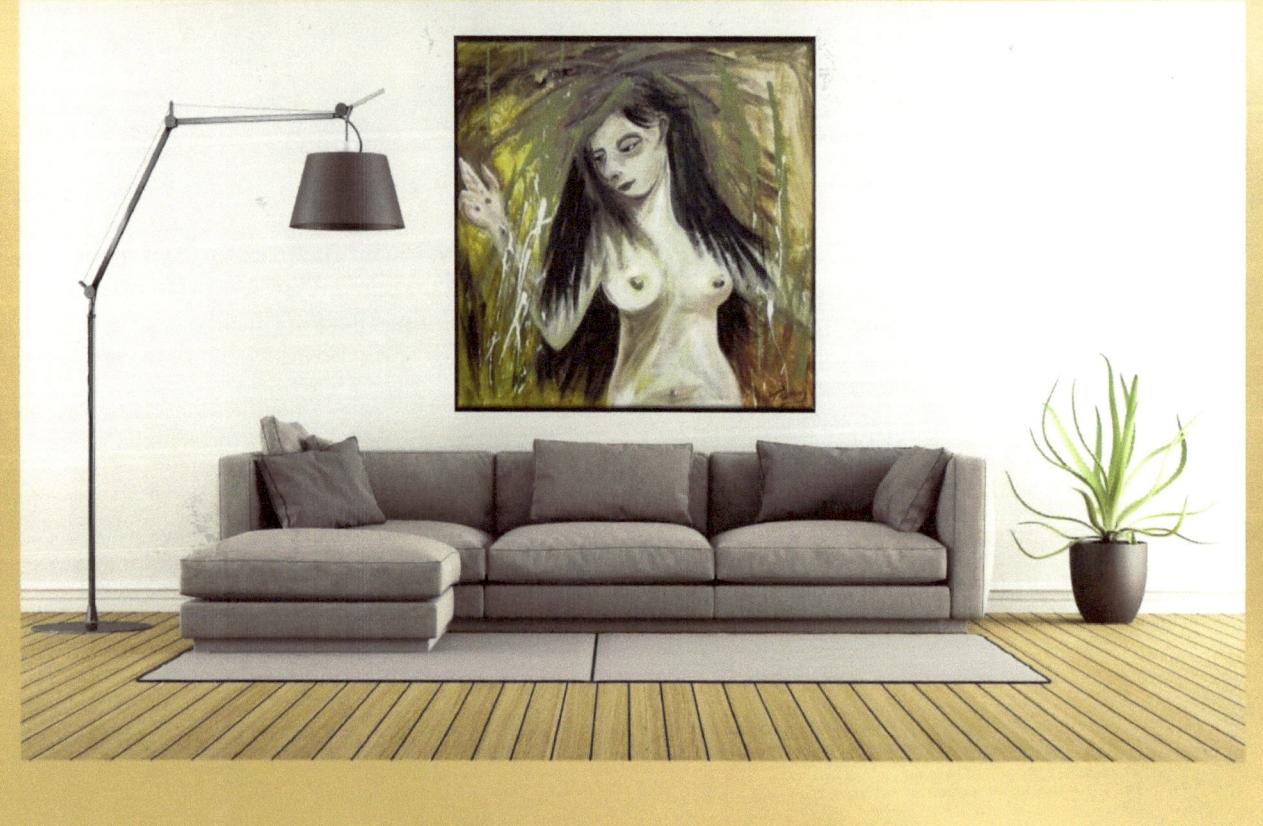

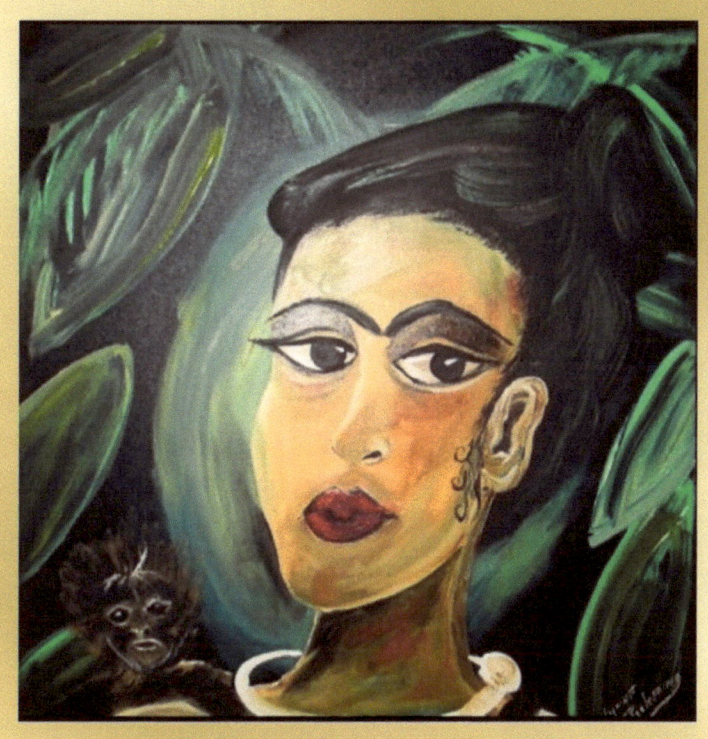

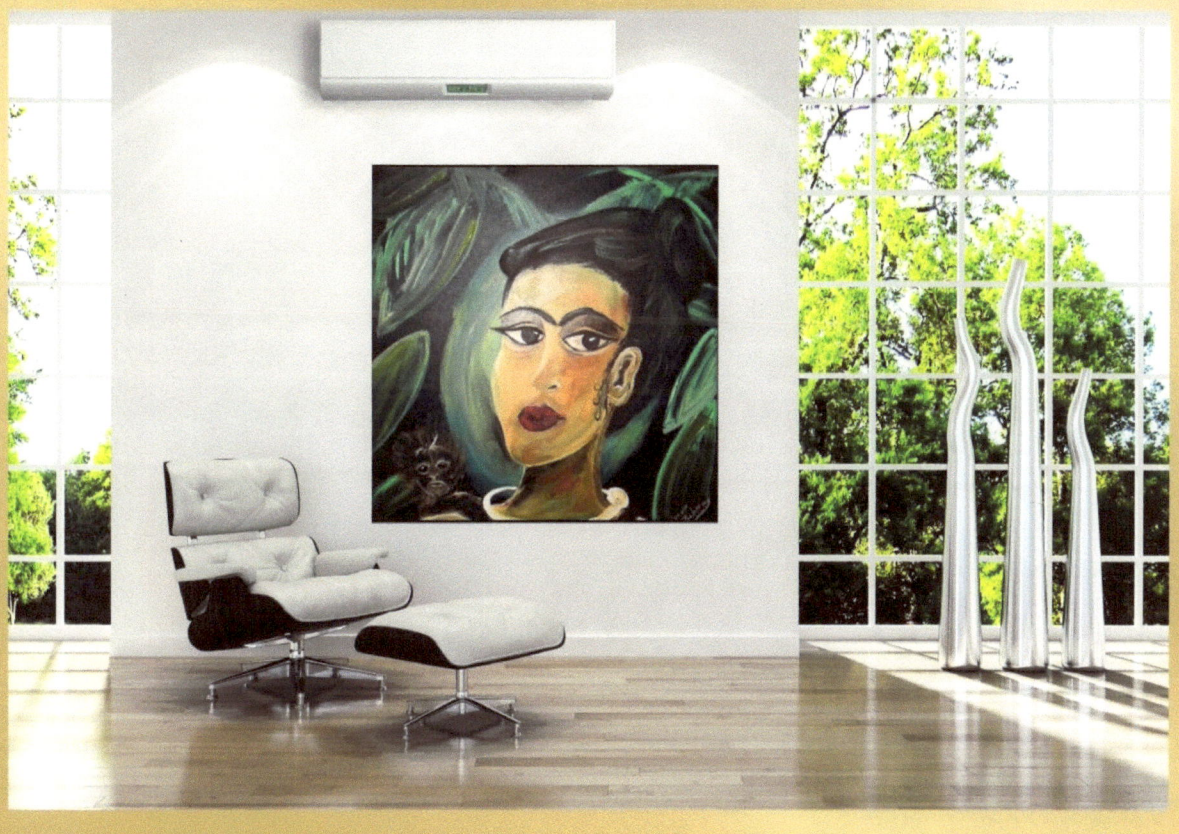

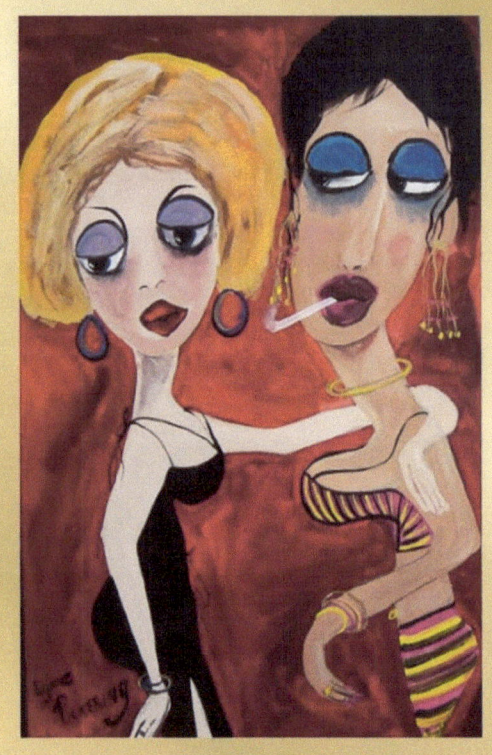
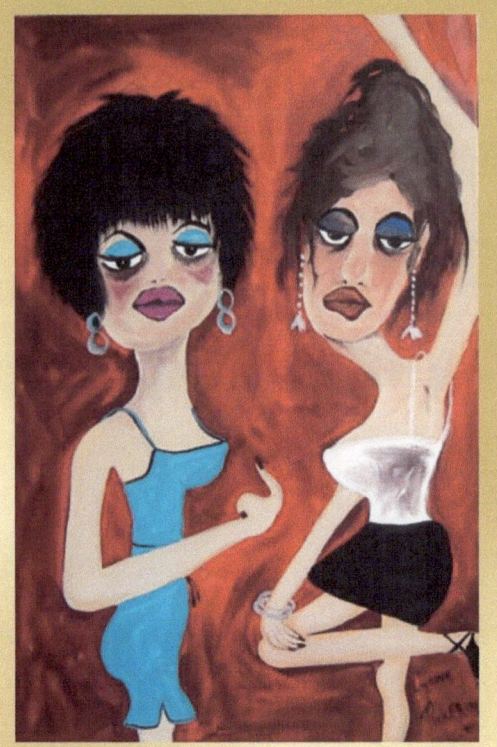
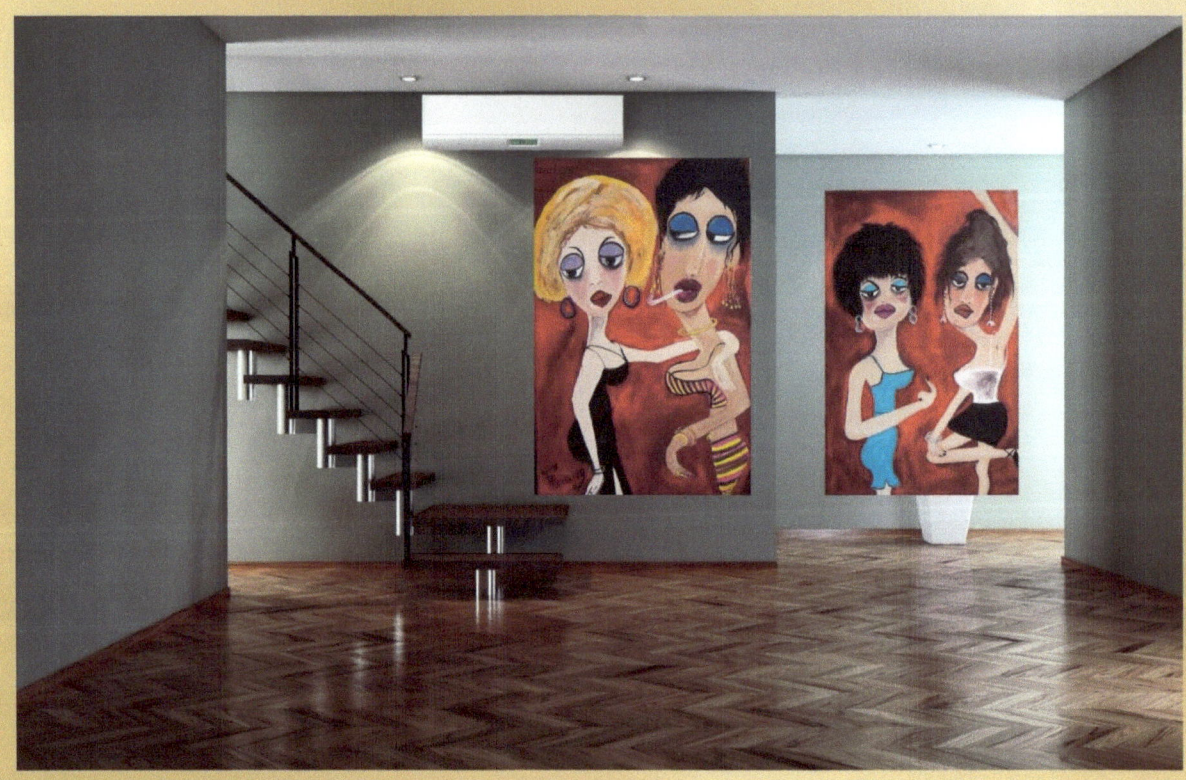

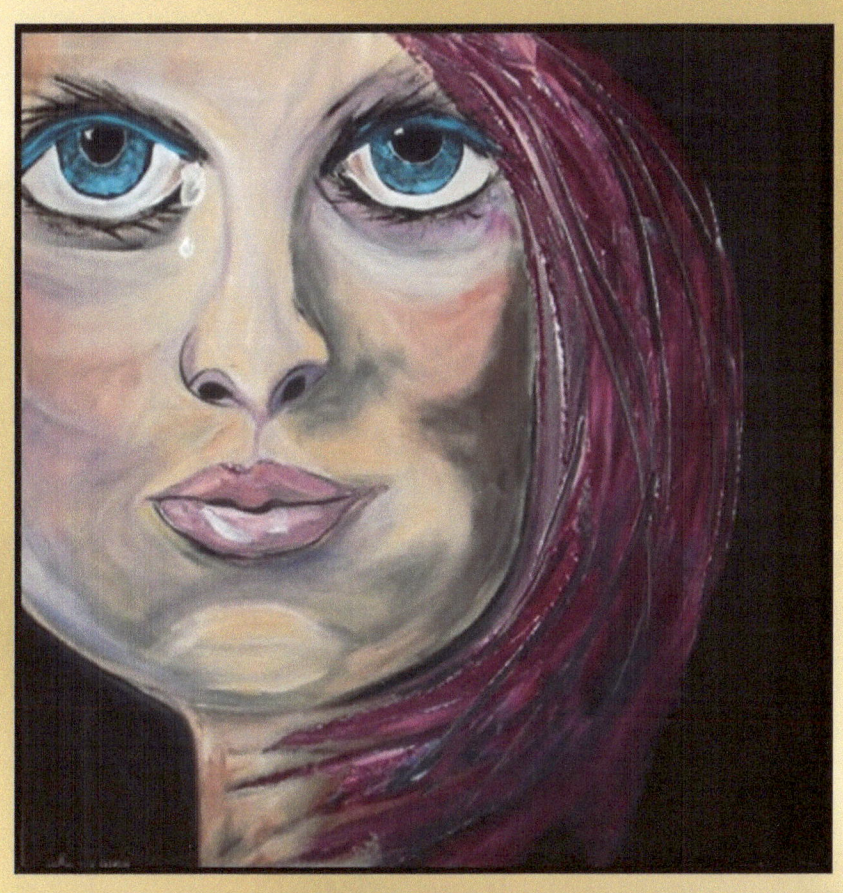

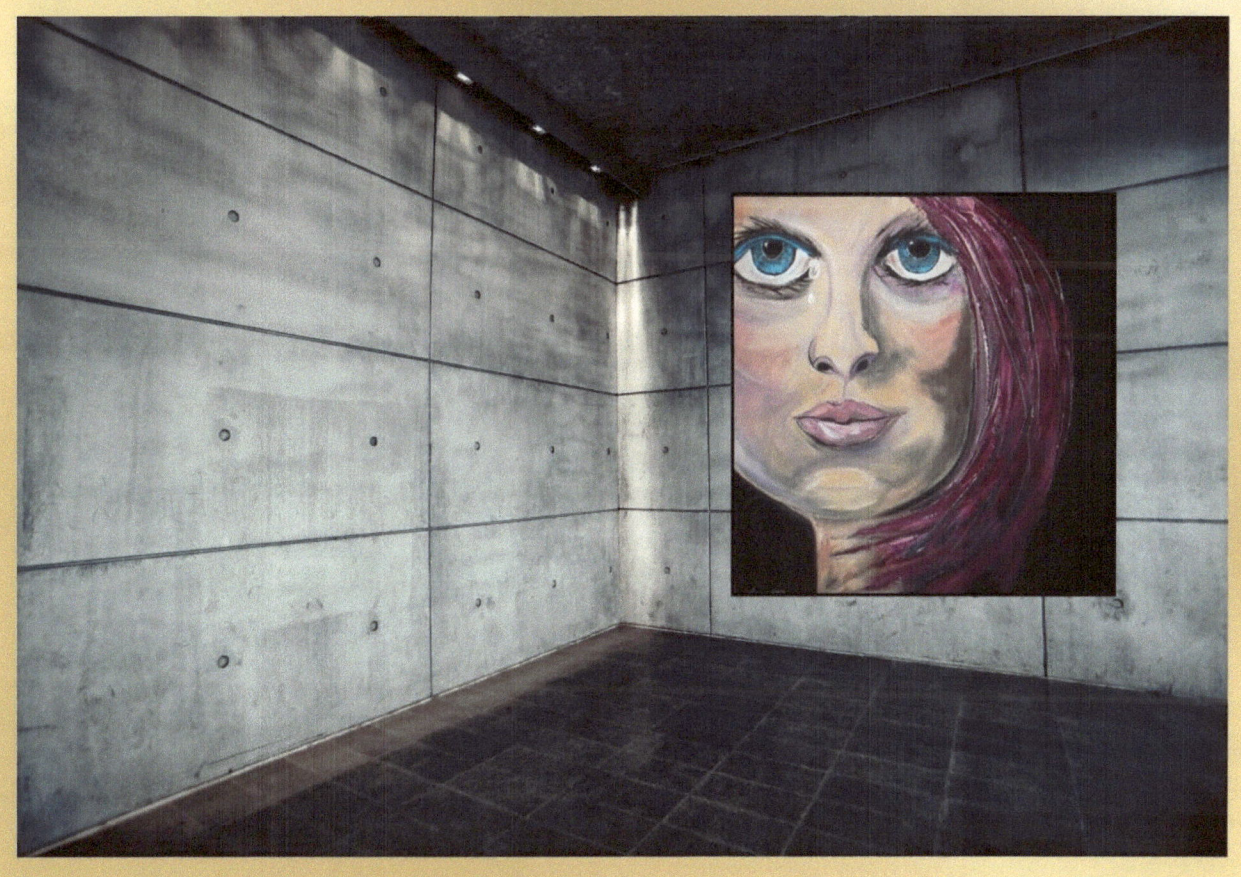

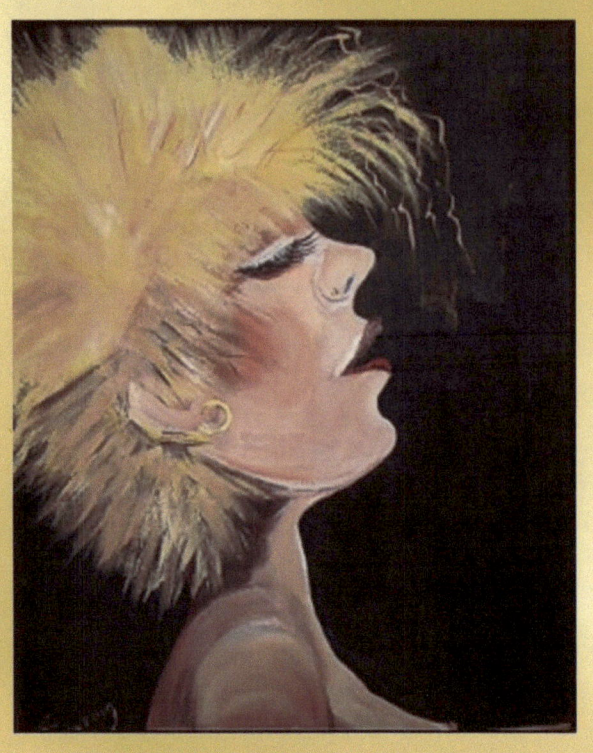

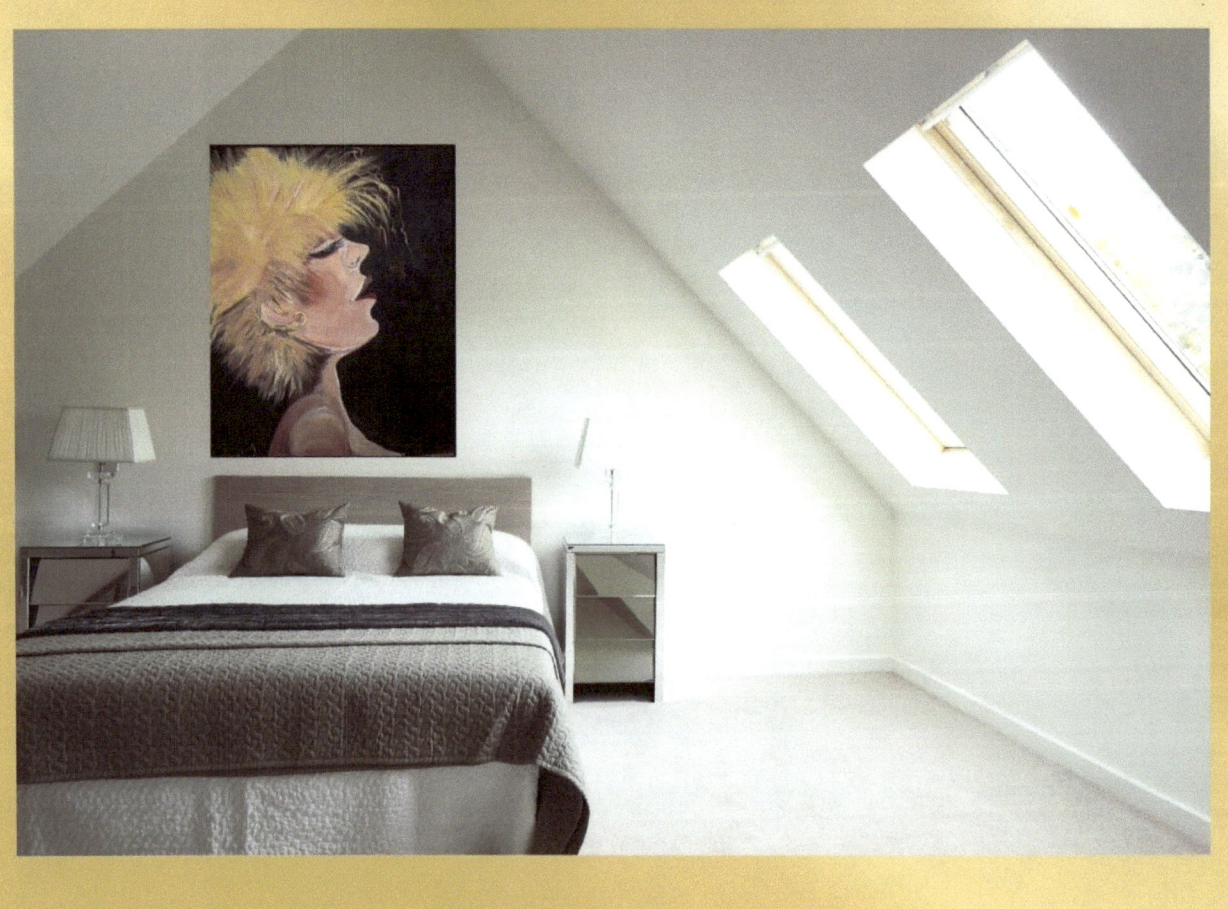

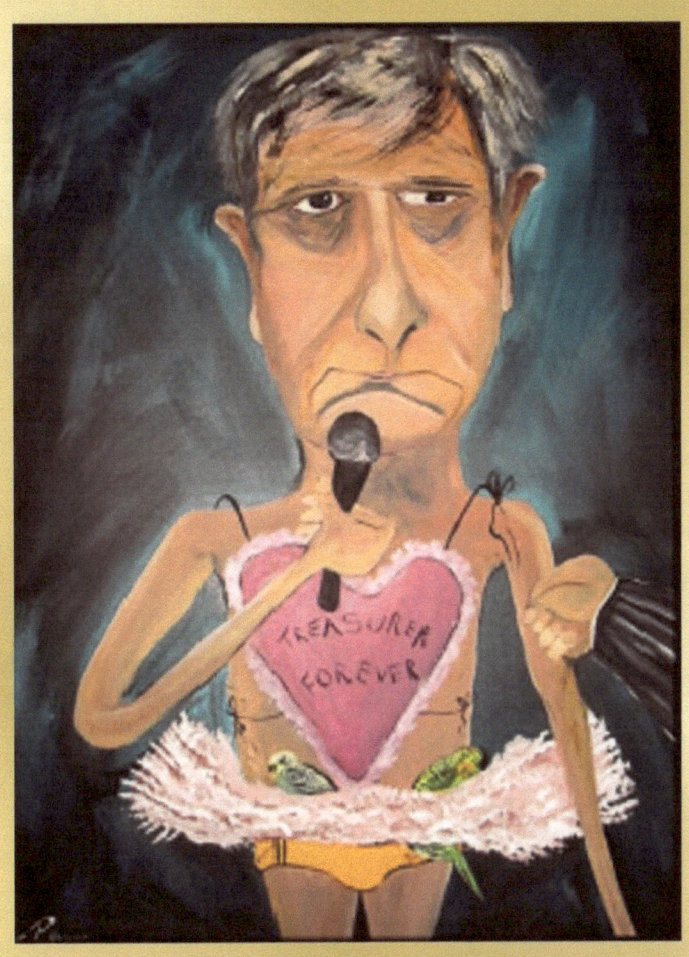

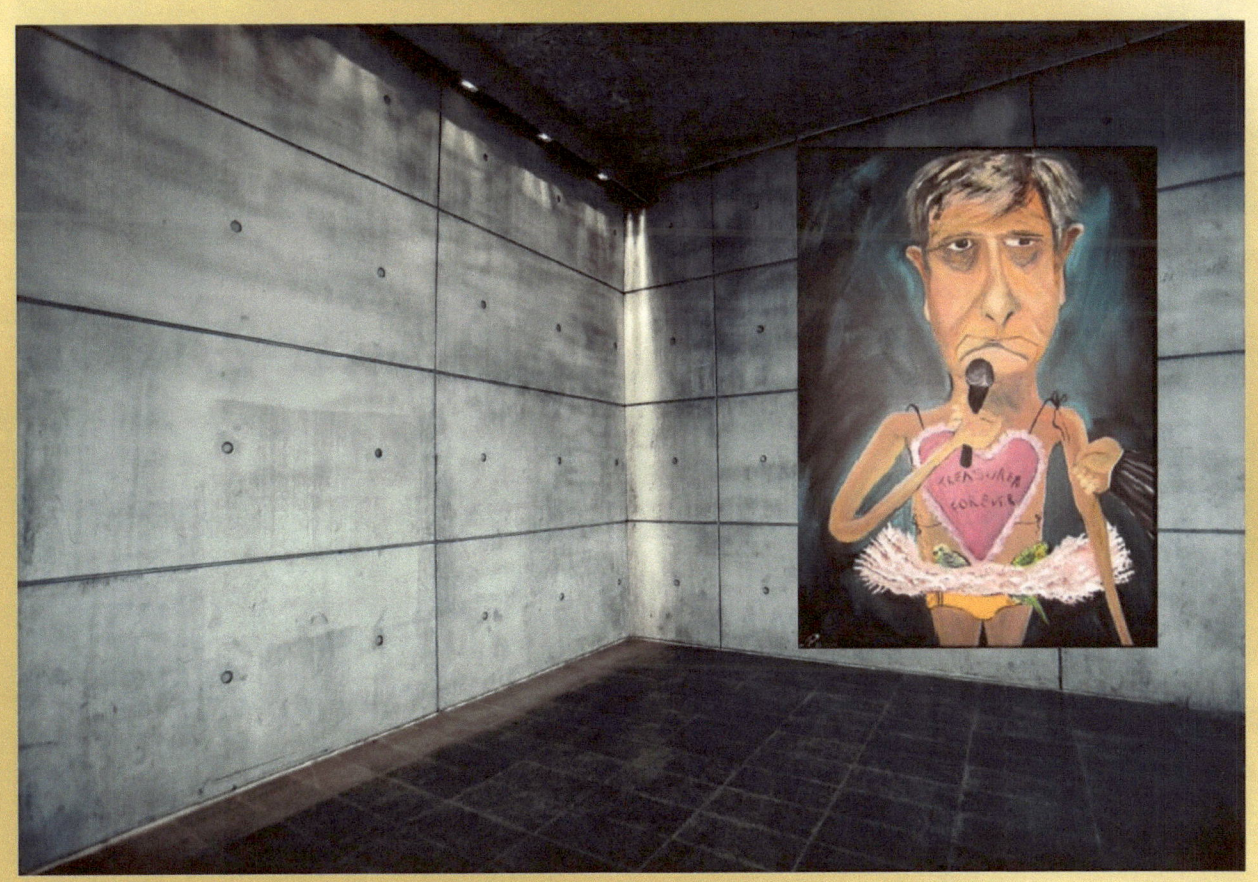

9

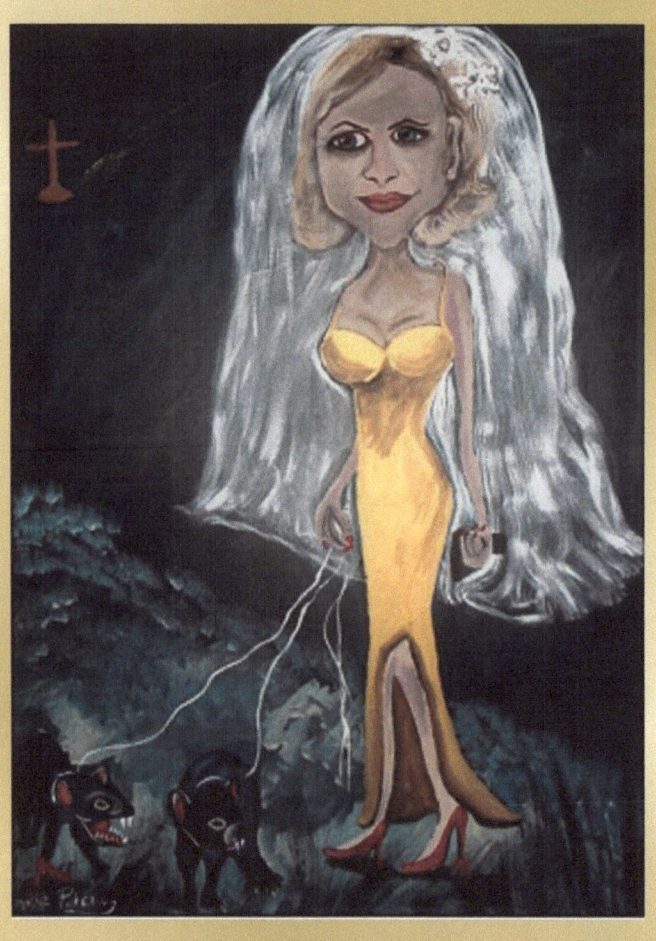

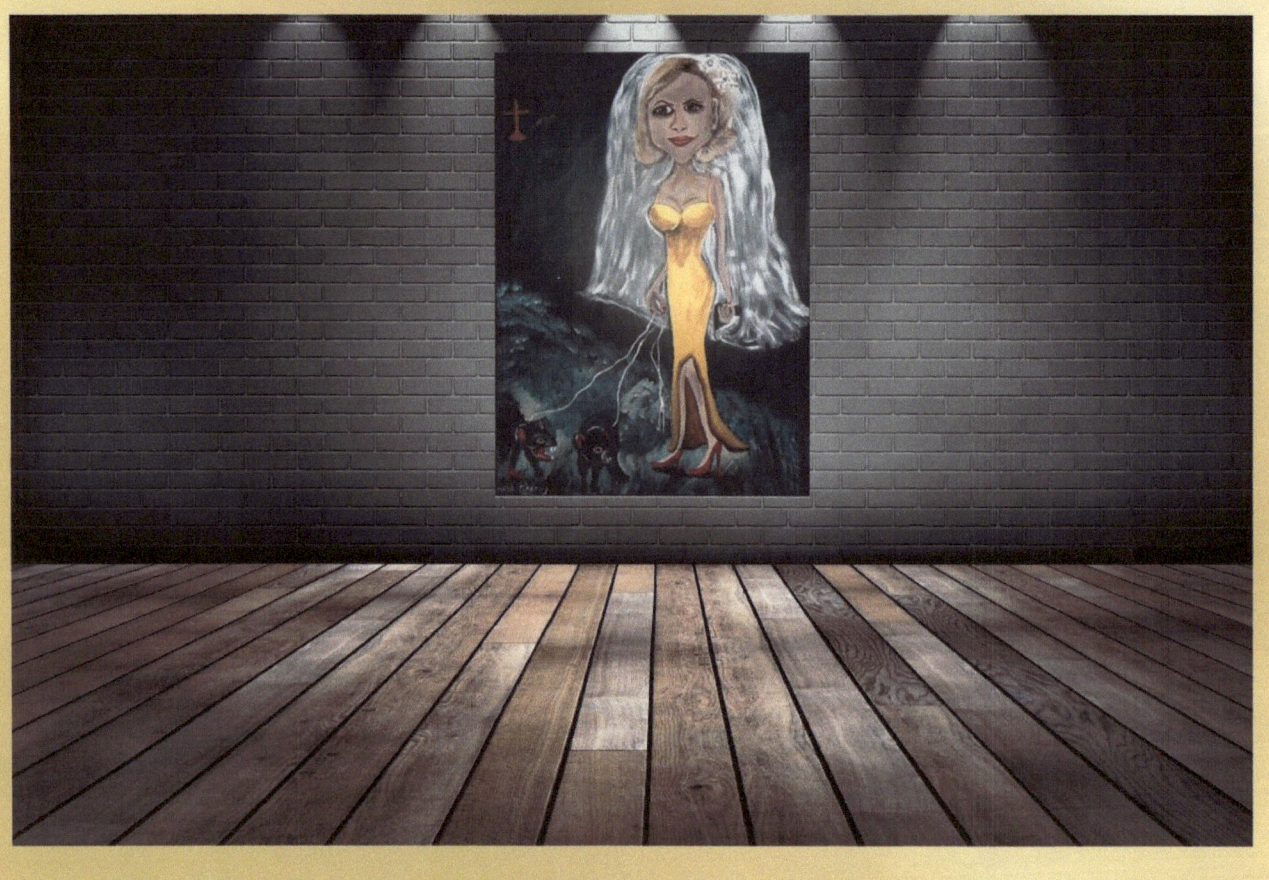

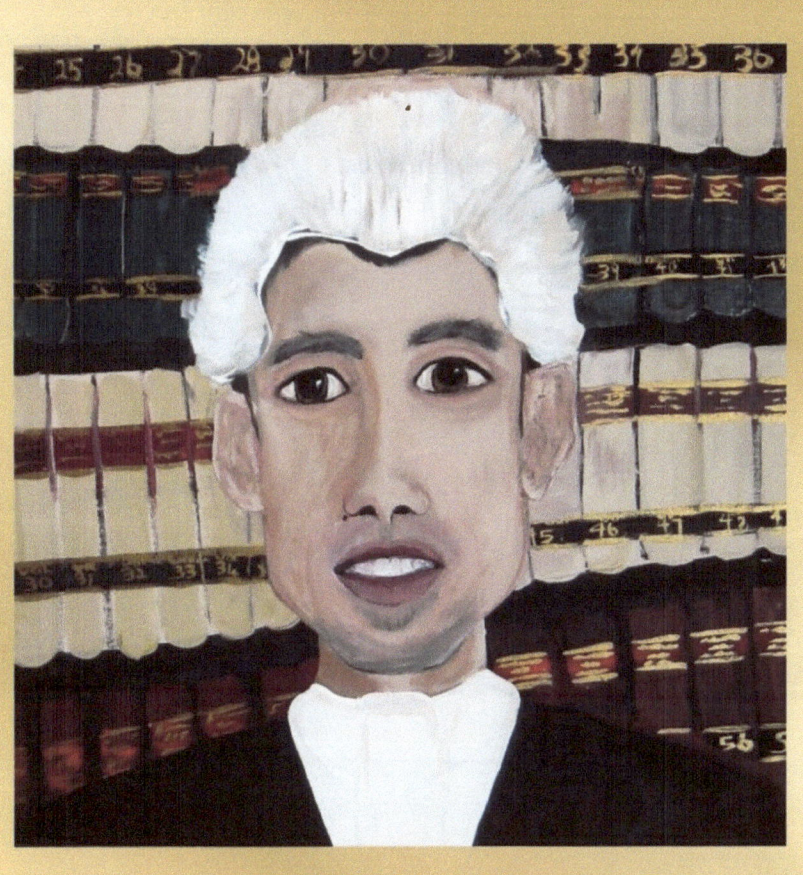

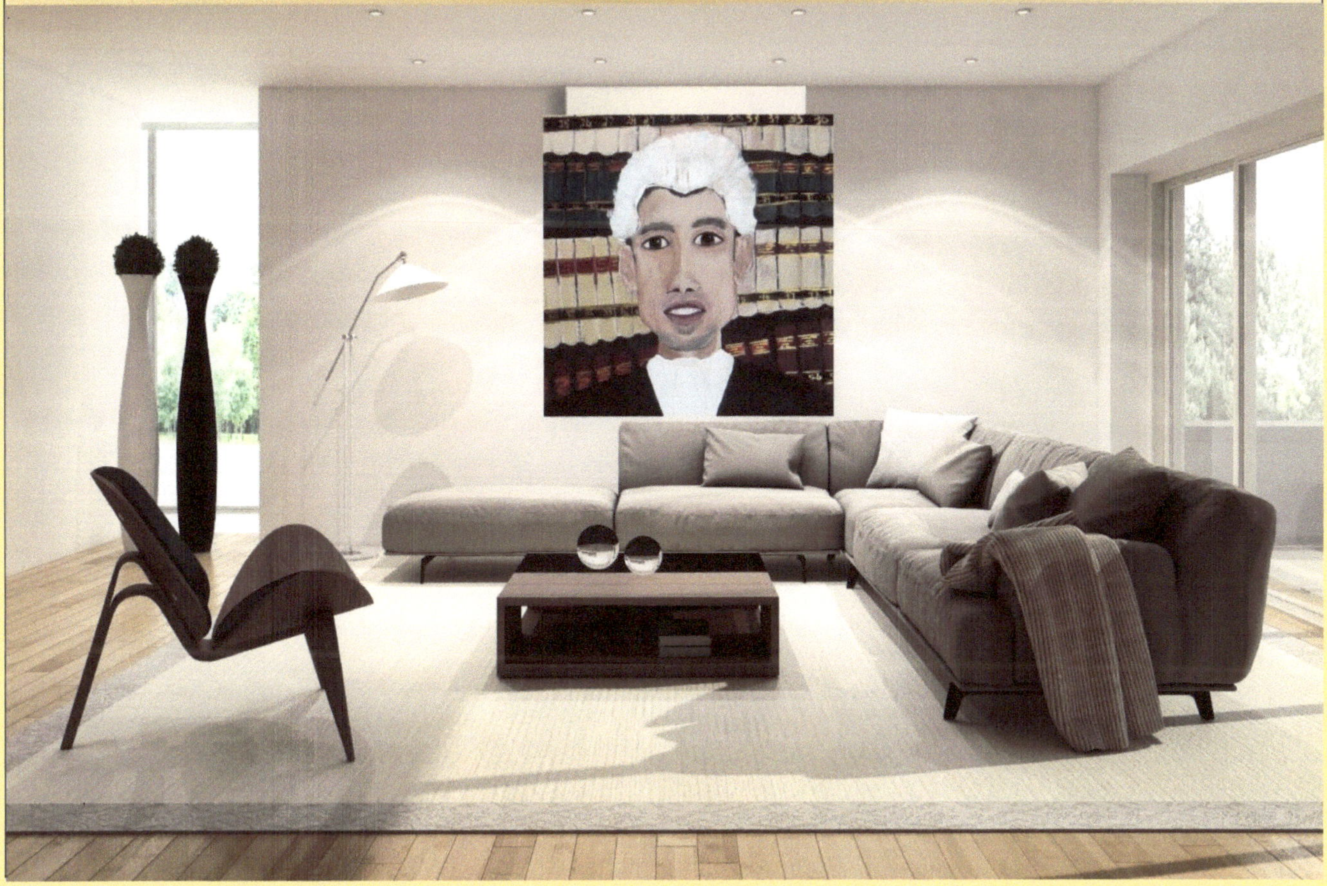

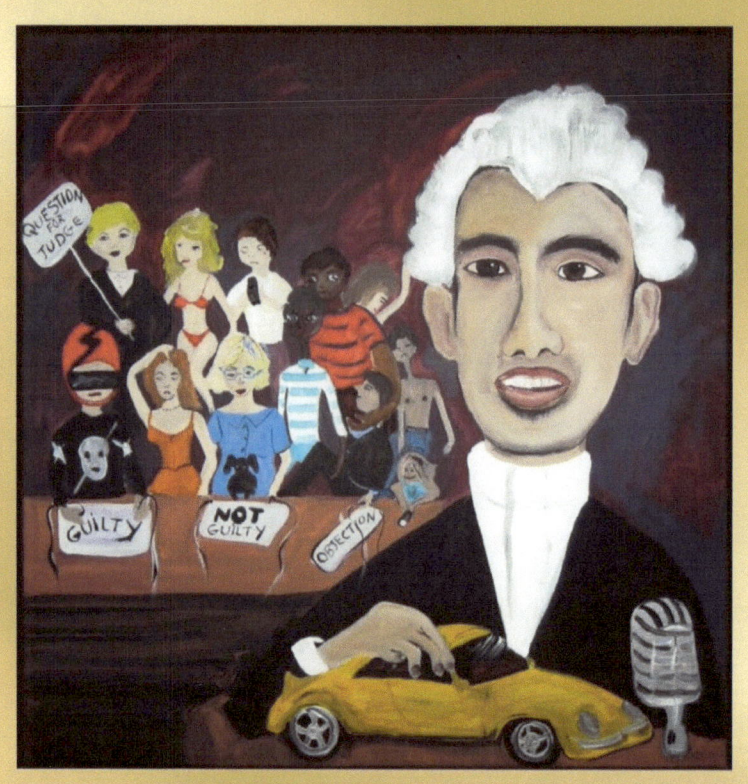

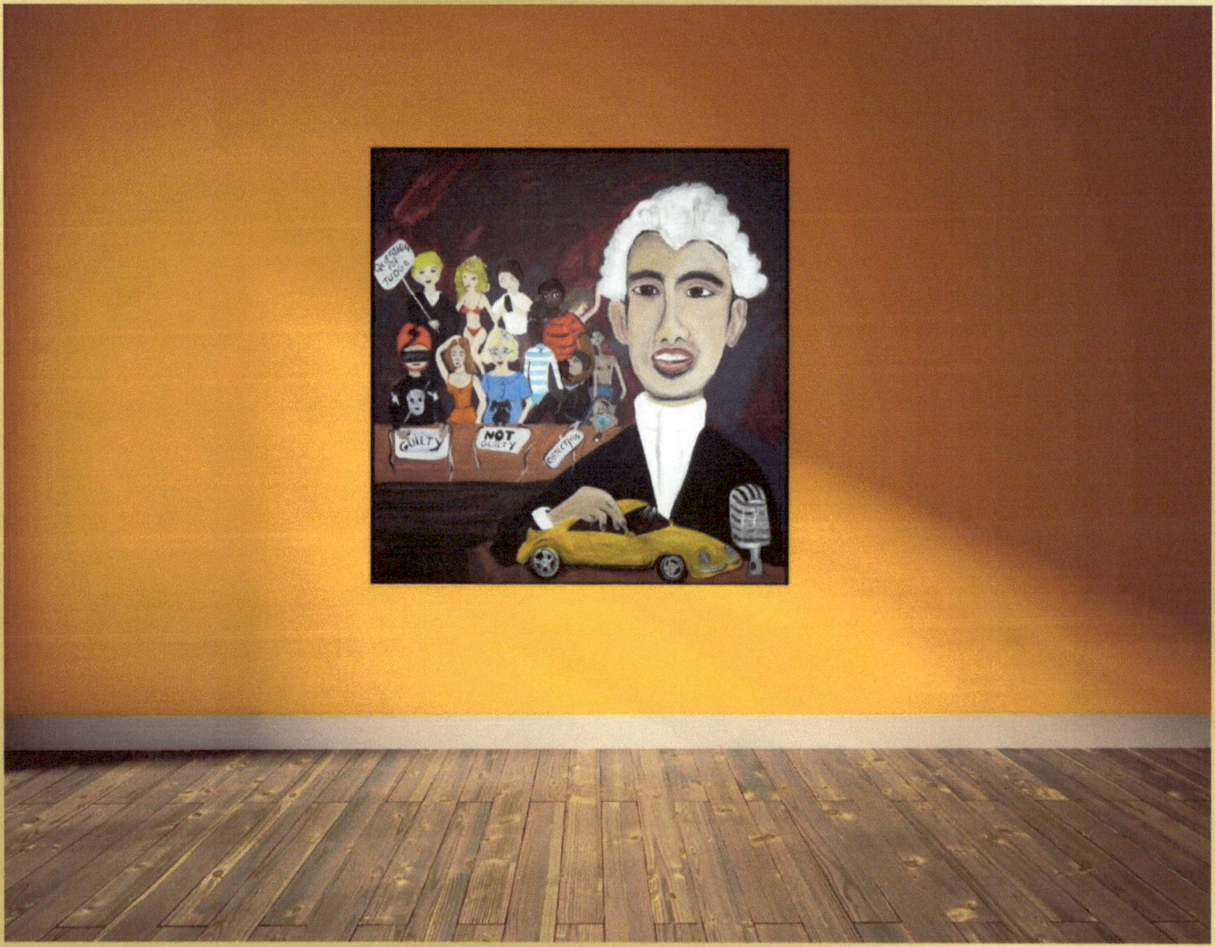

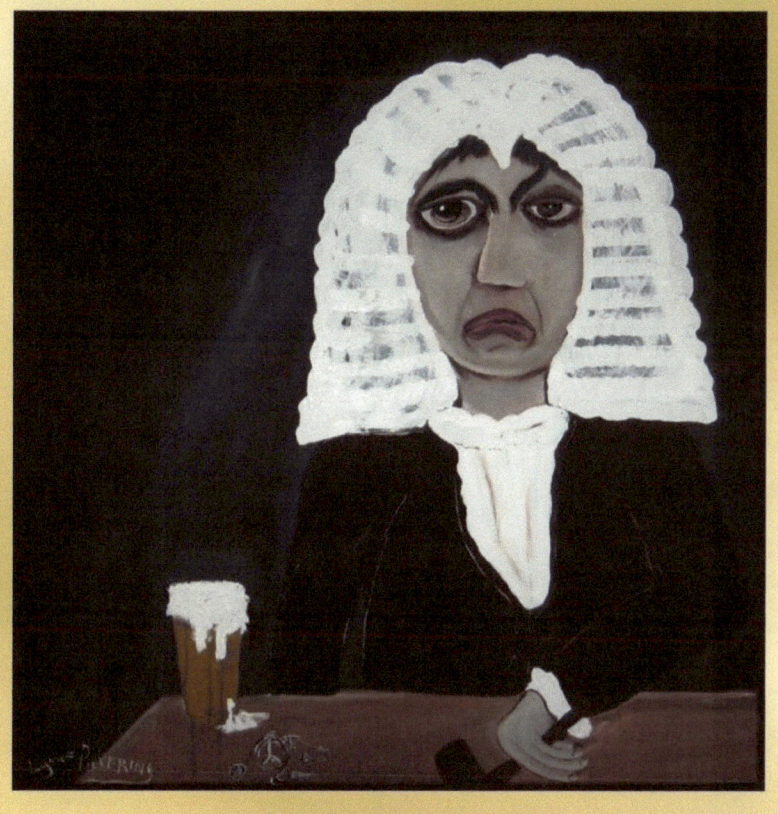

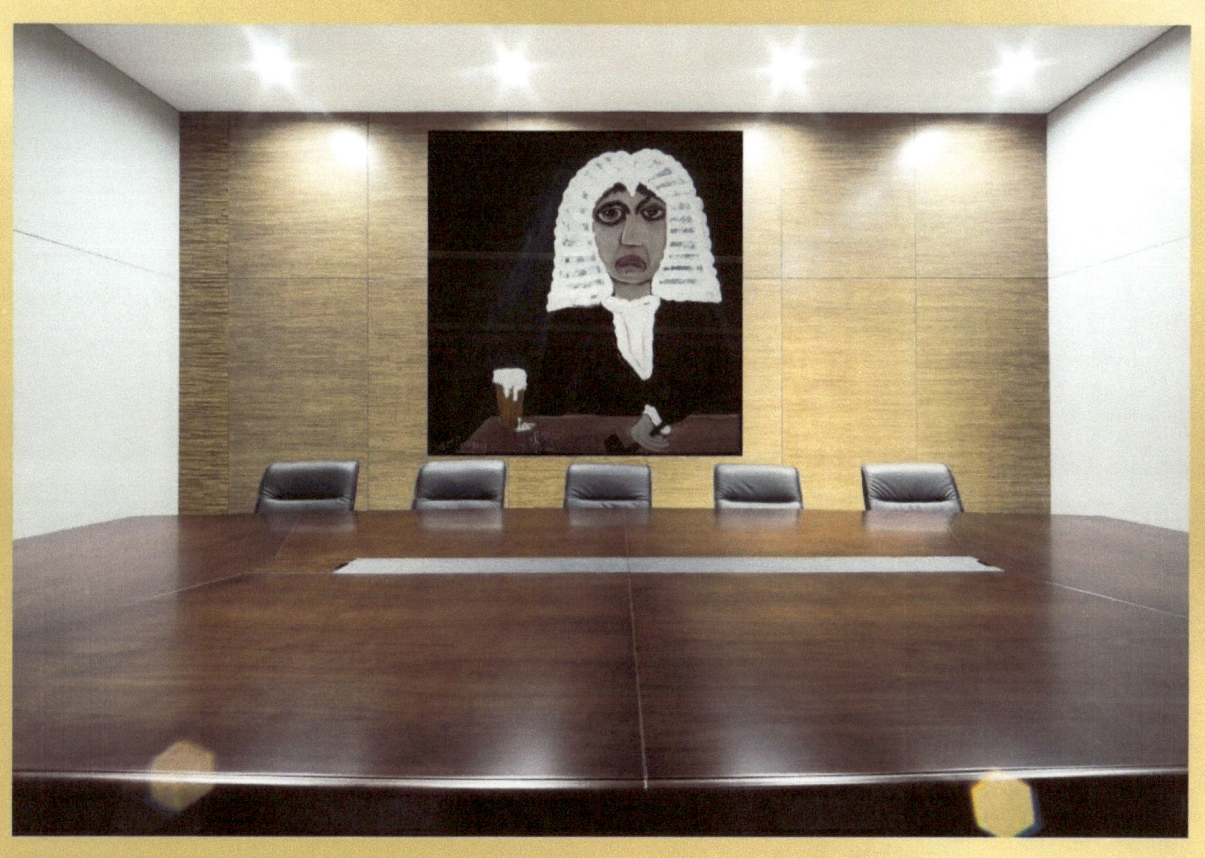

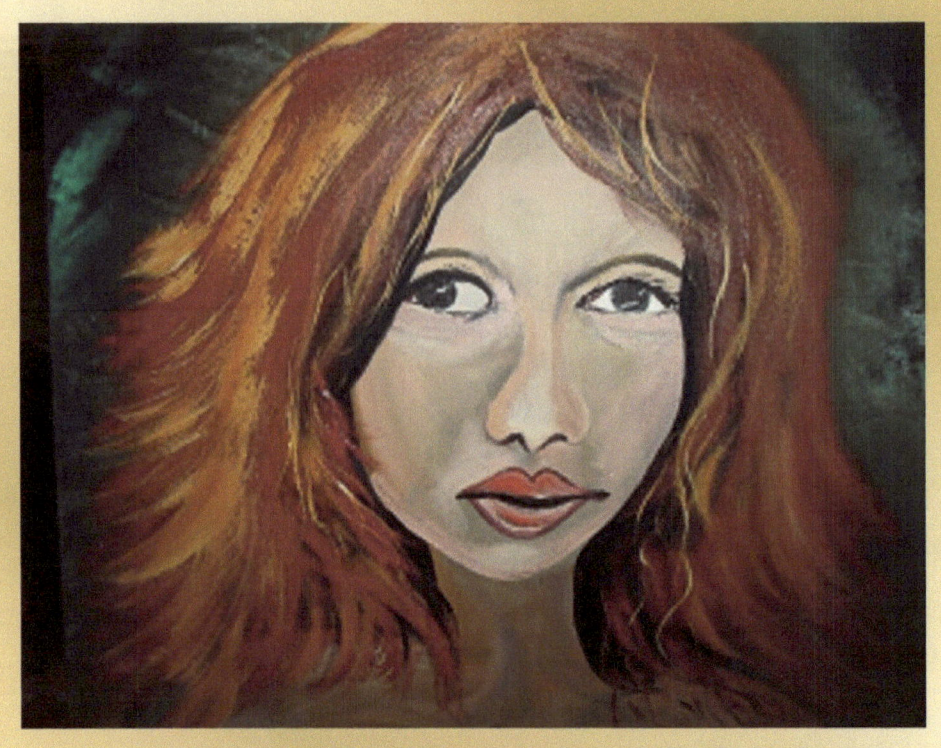

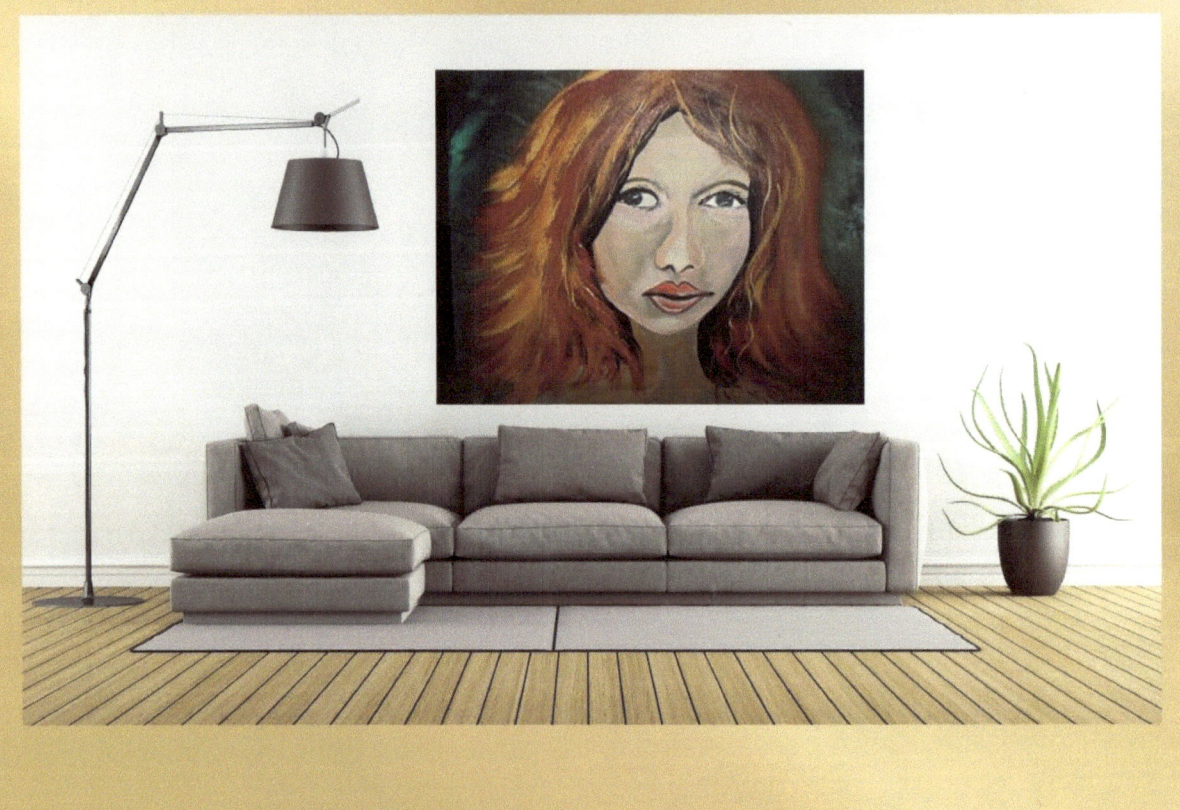

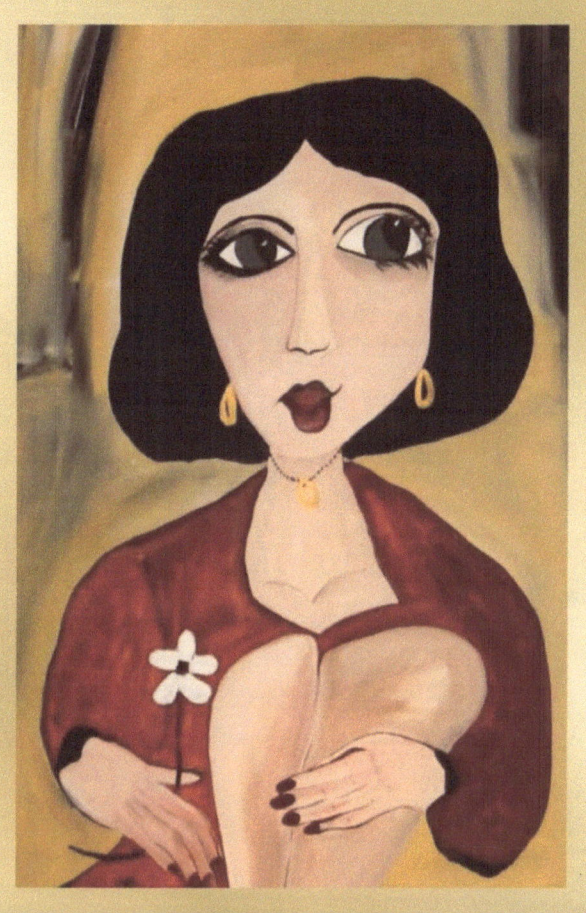

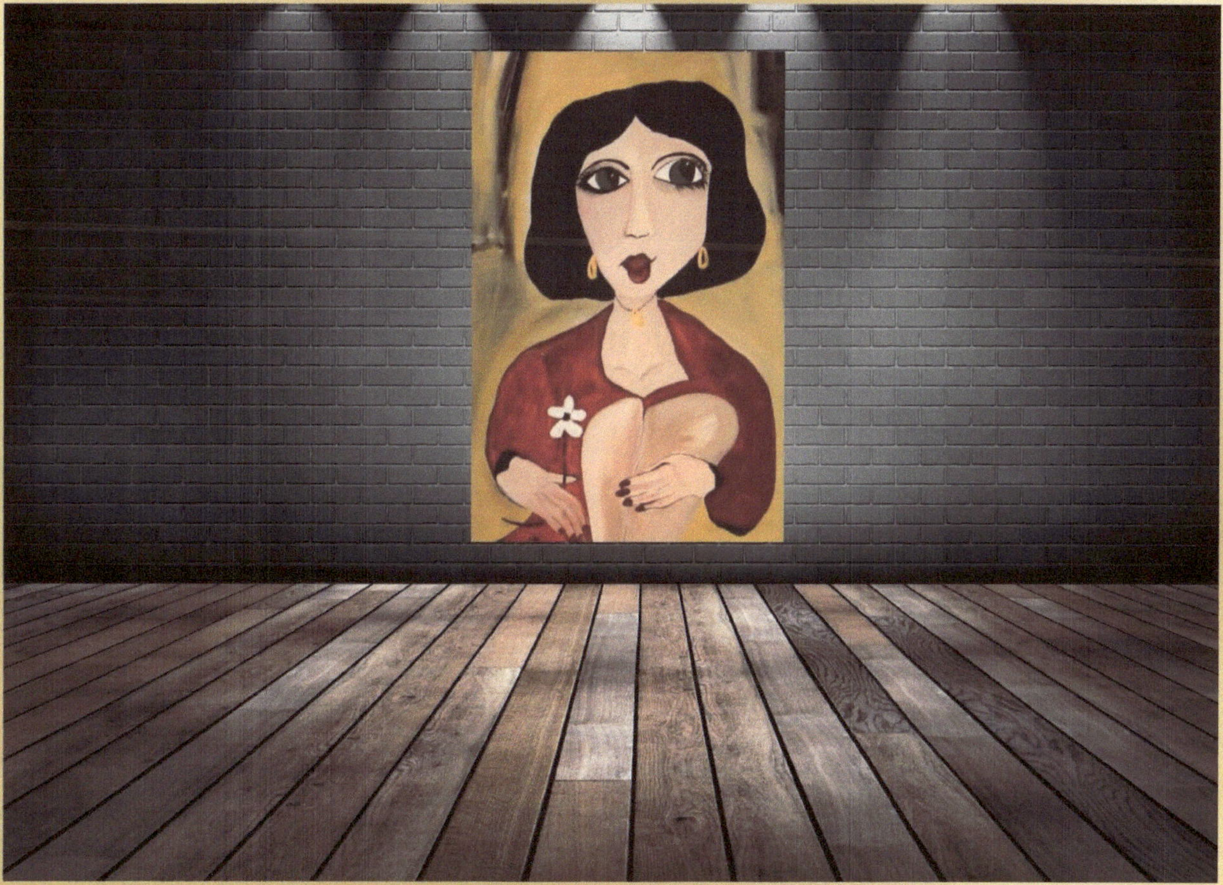

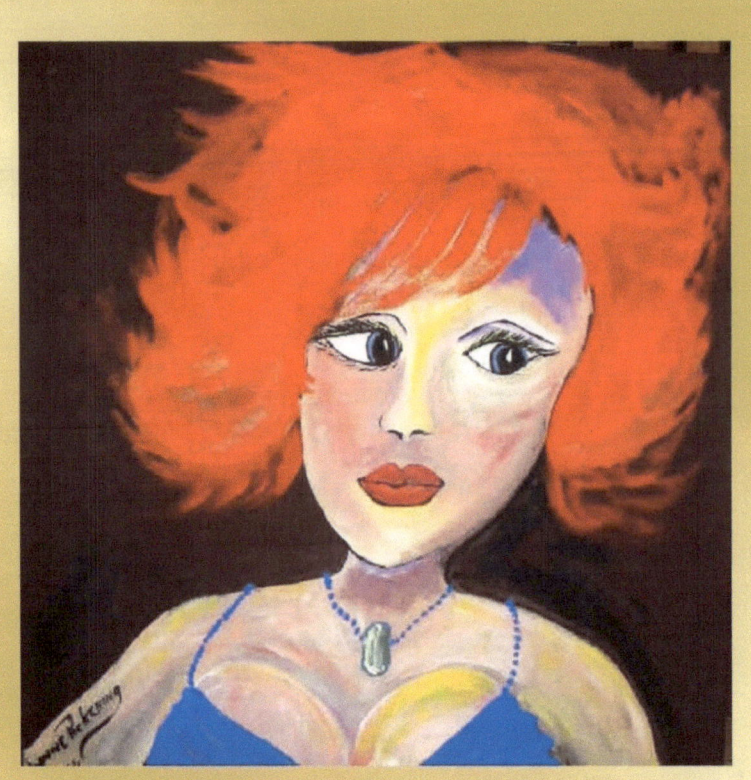

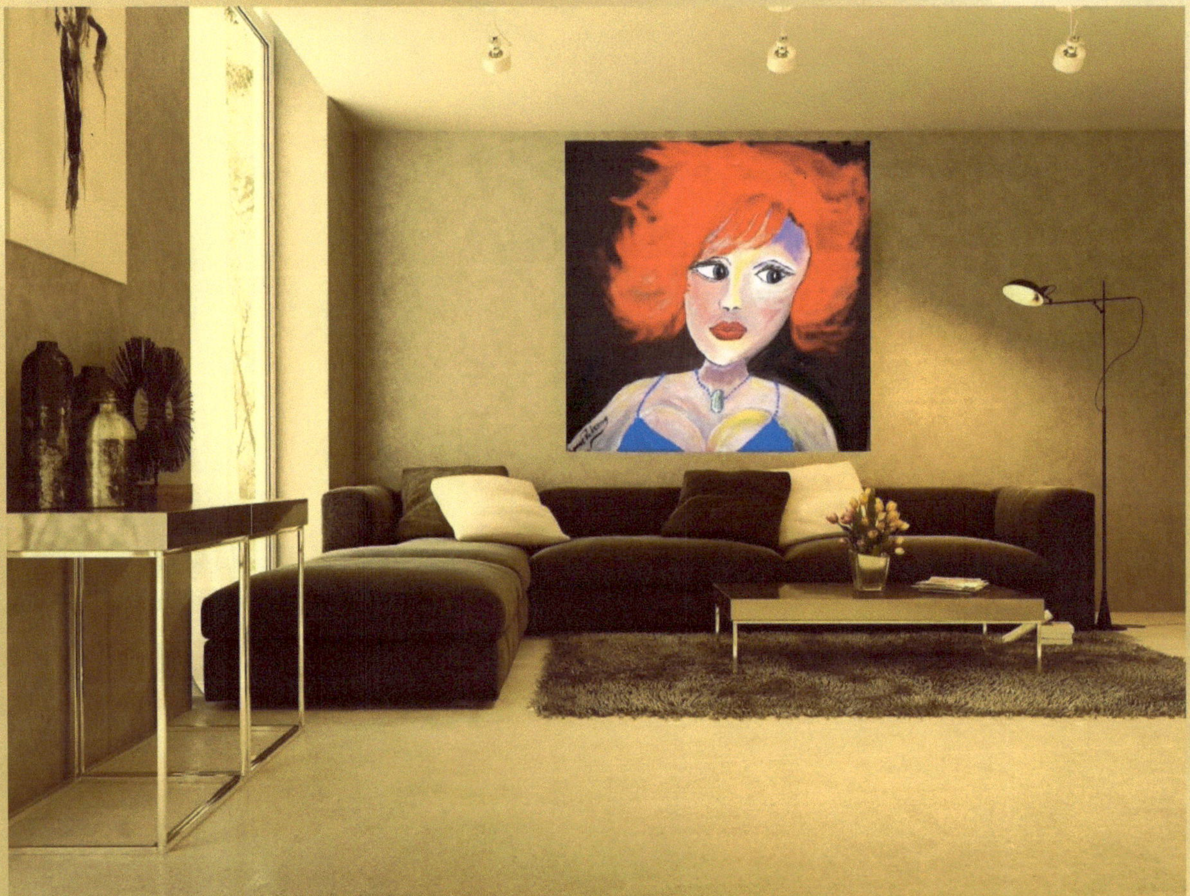

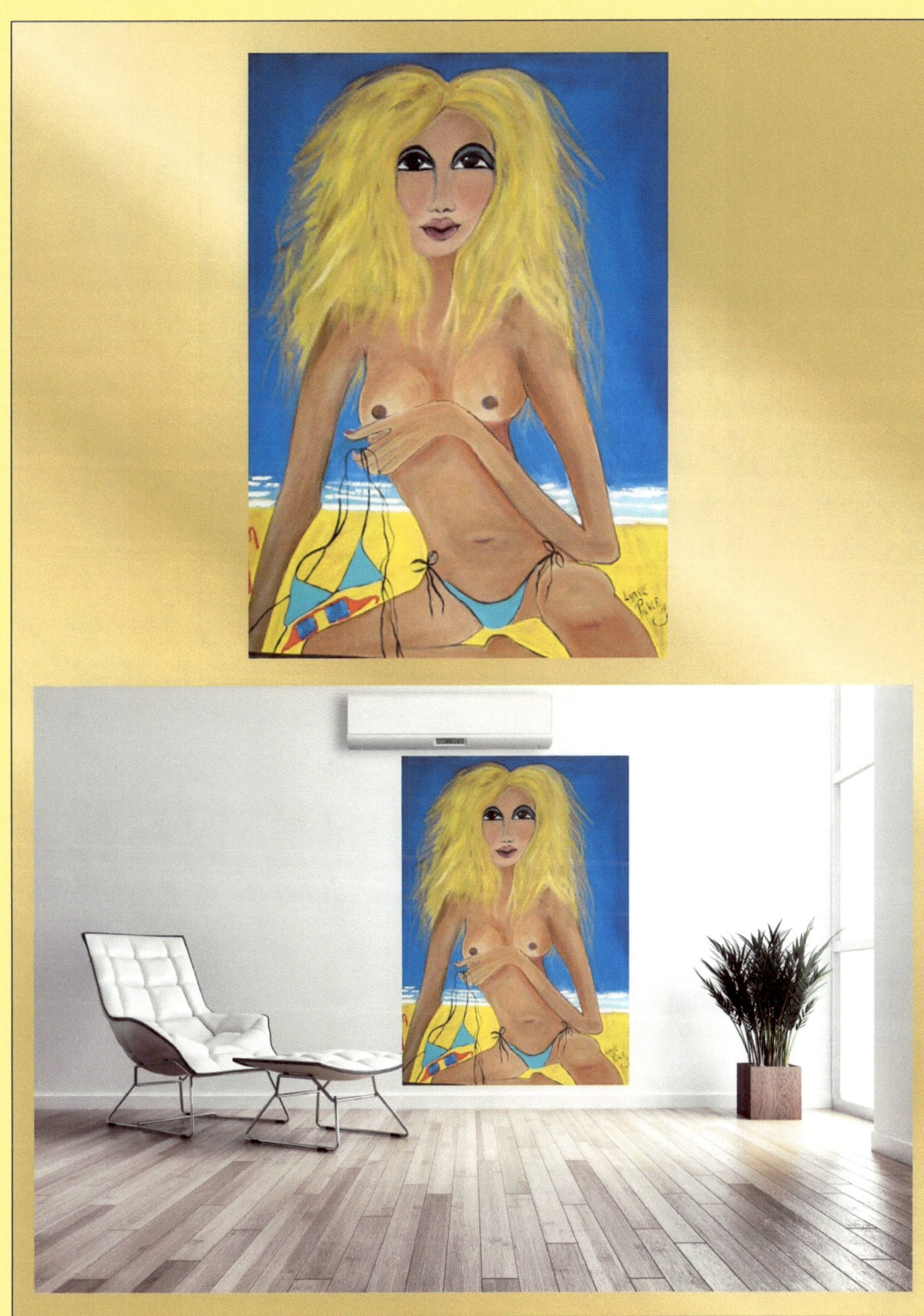

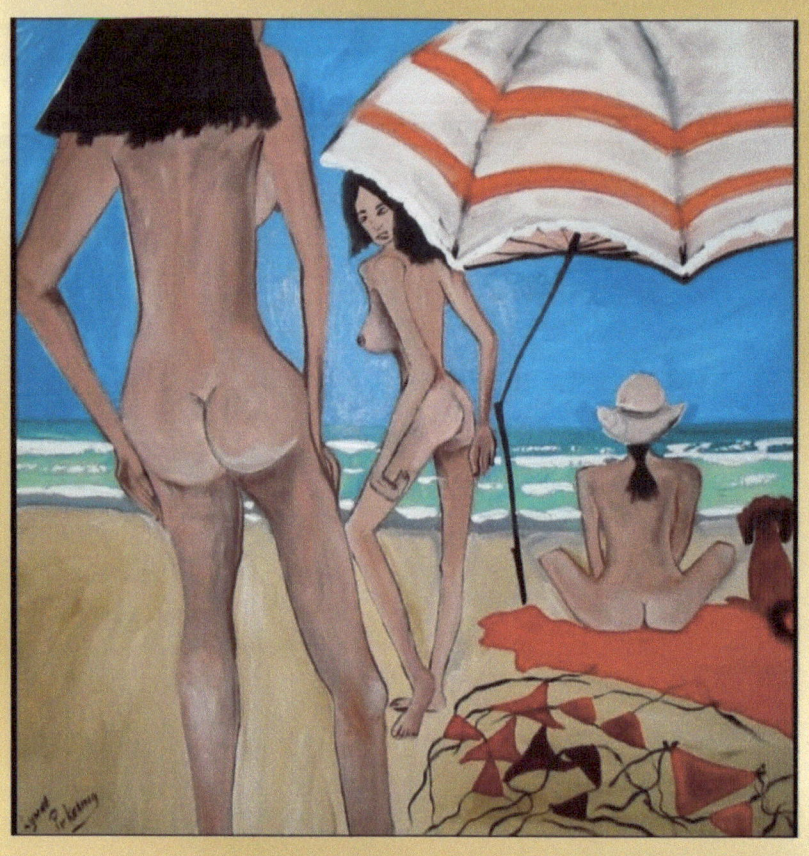

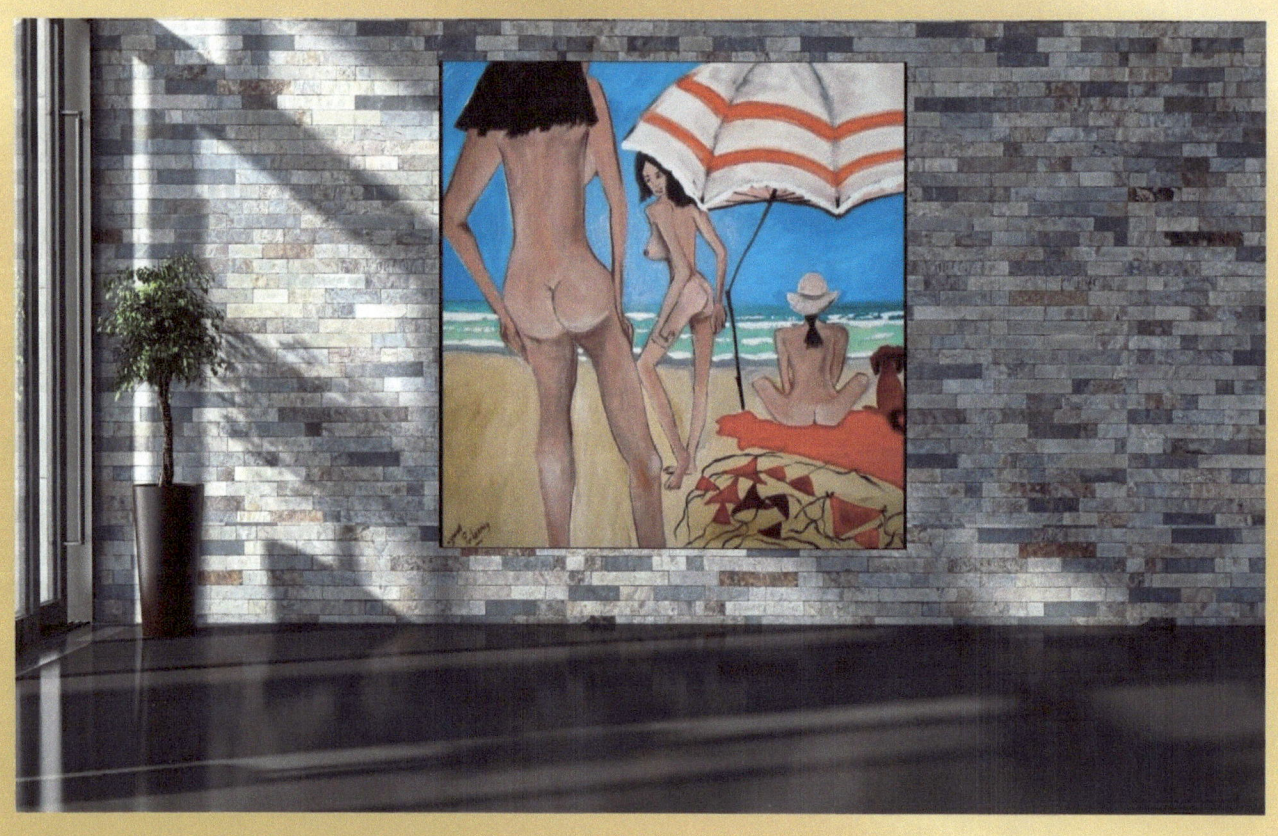

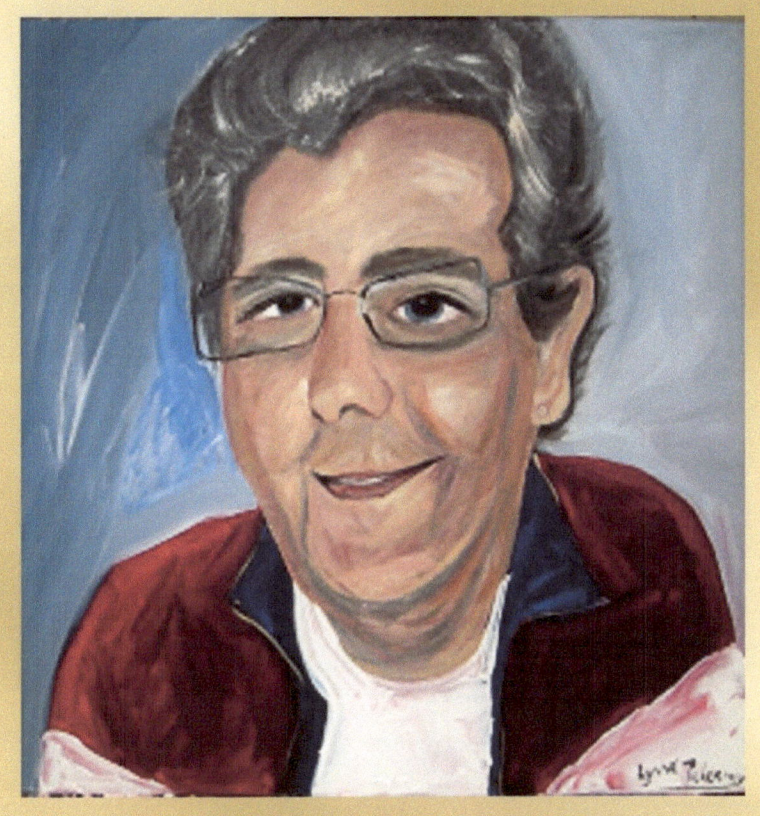

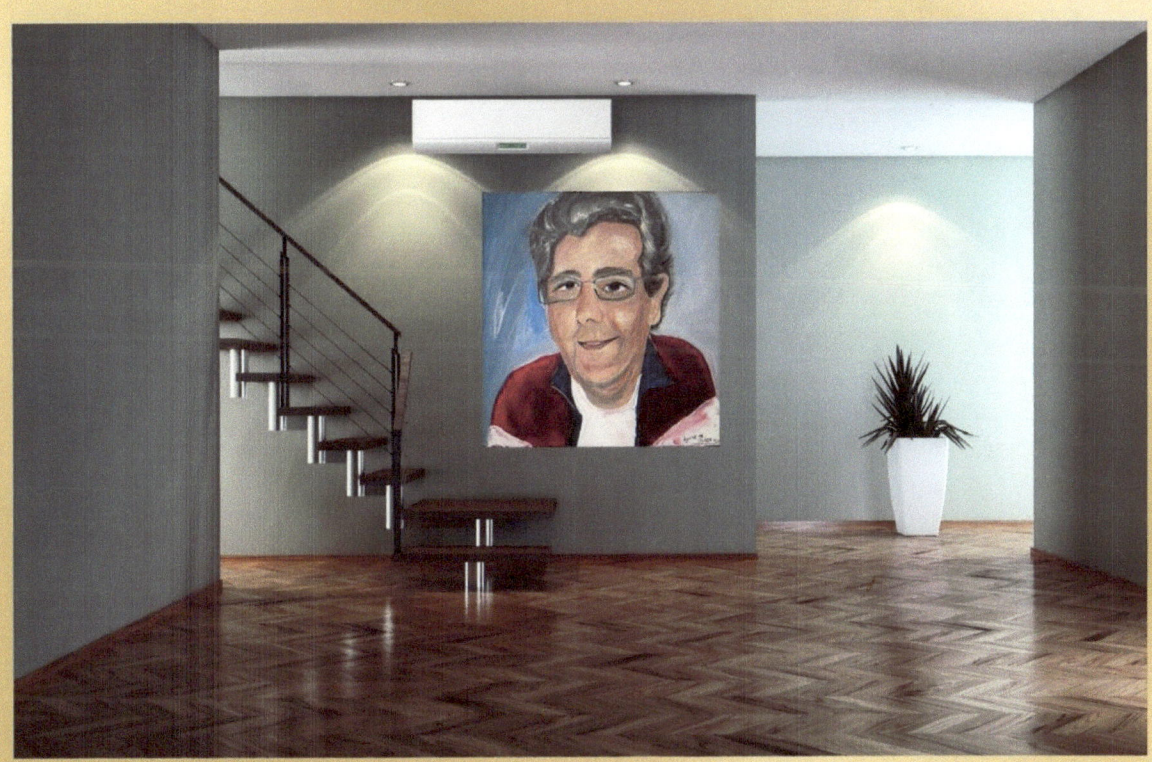

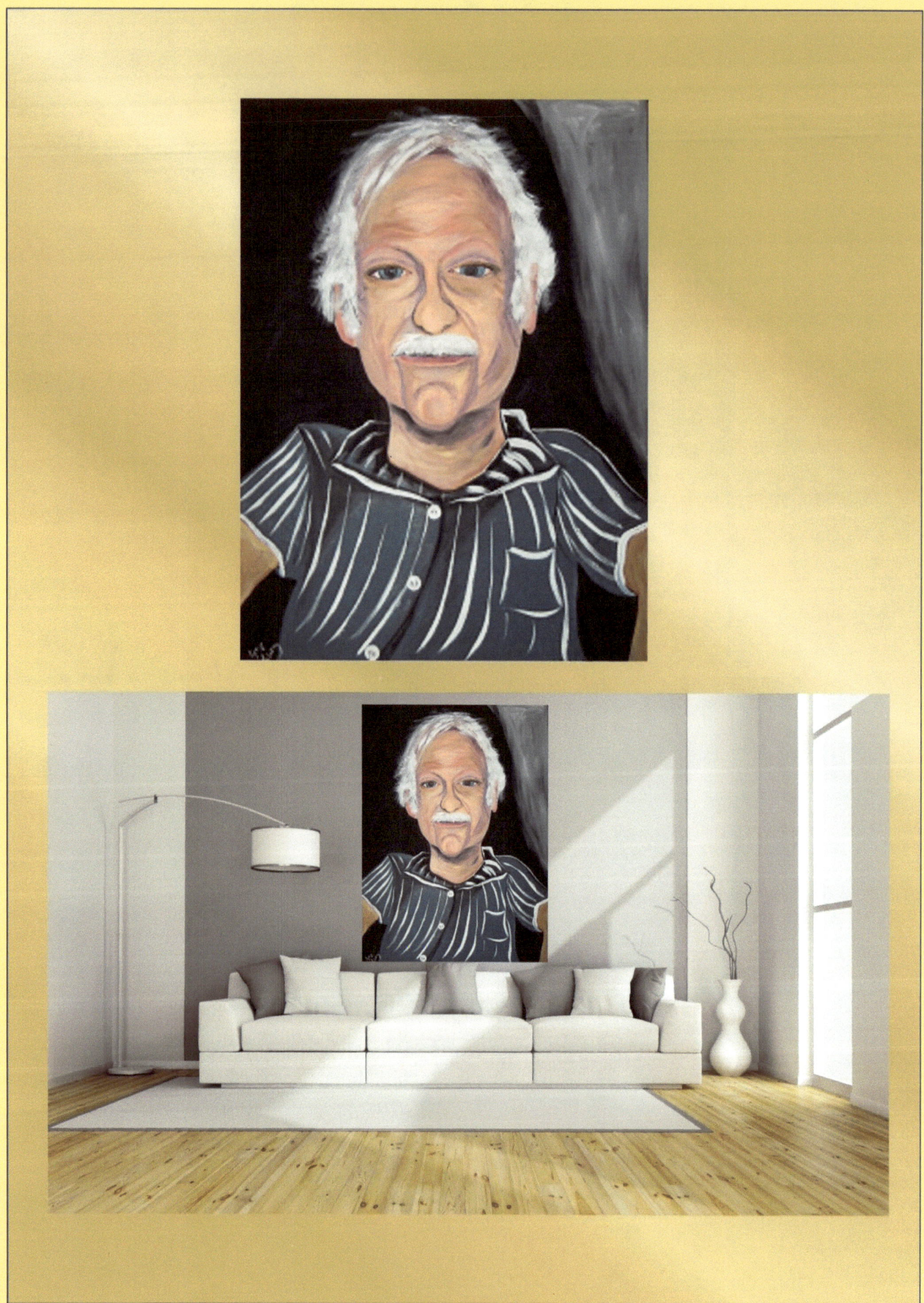

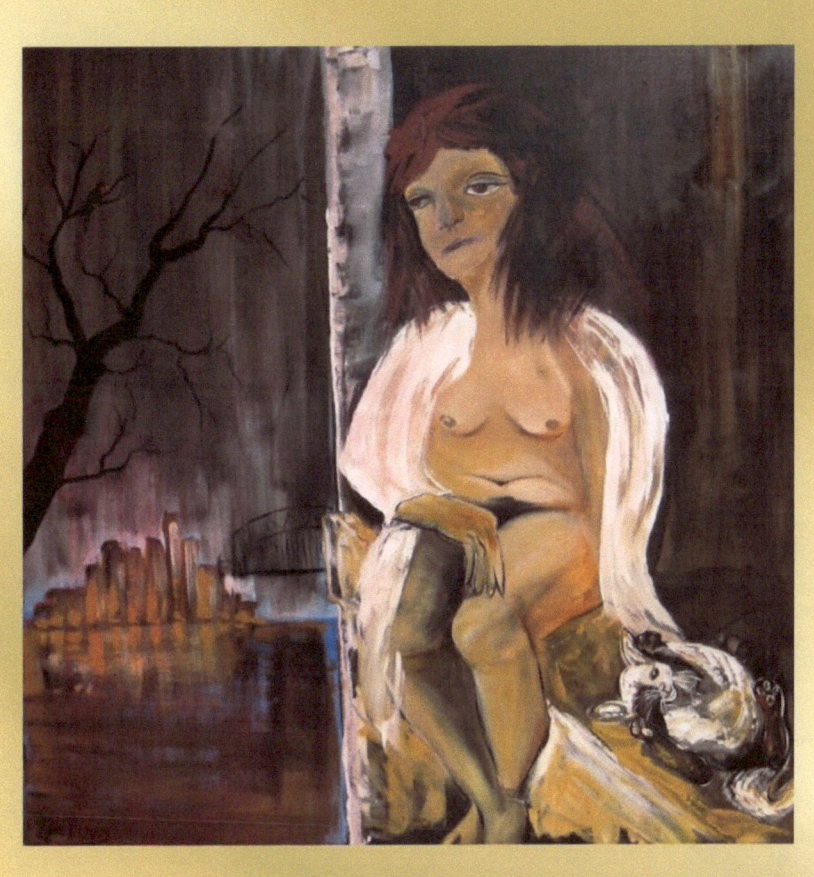

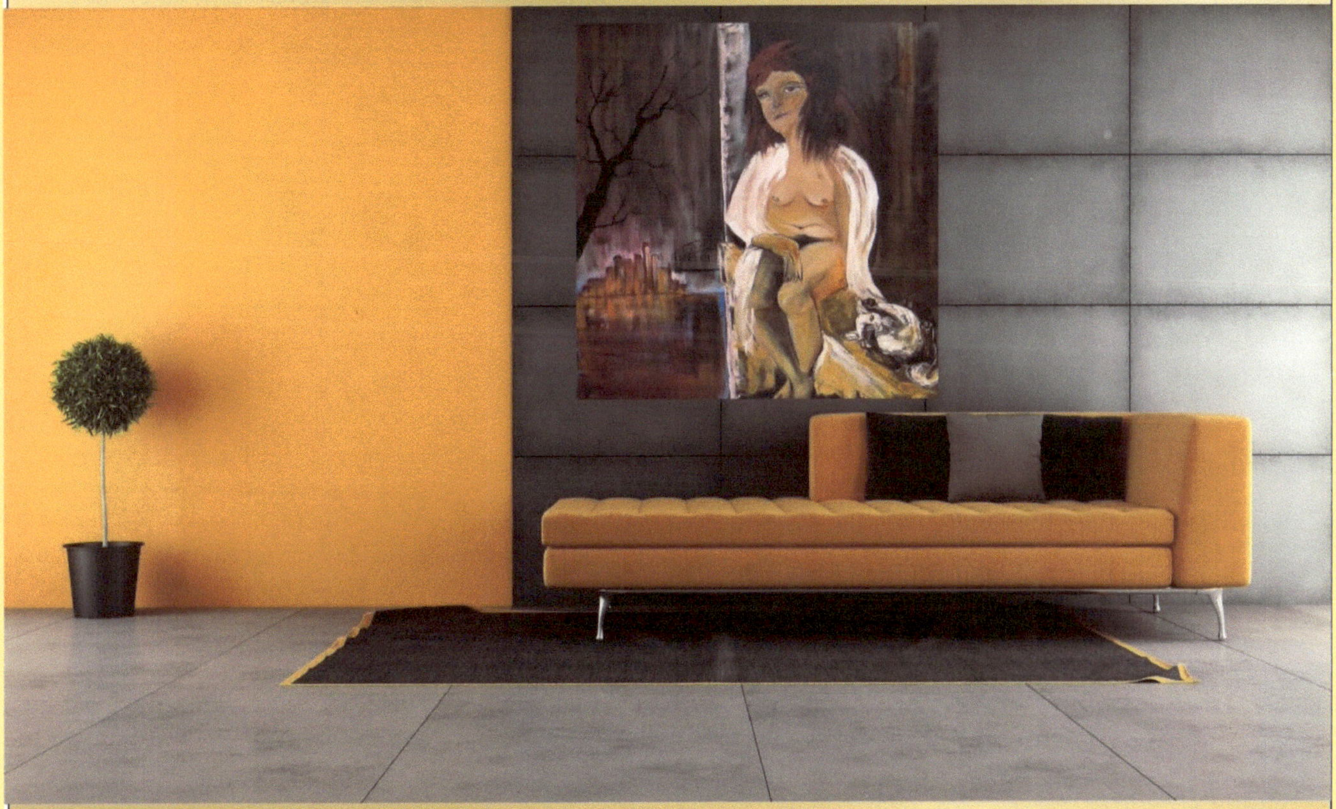

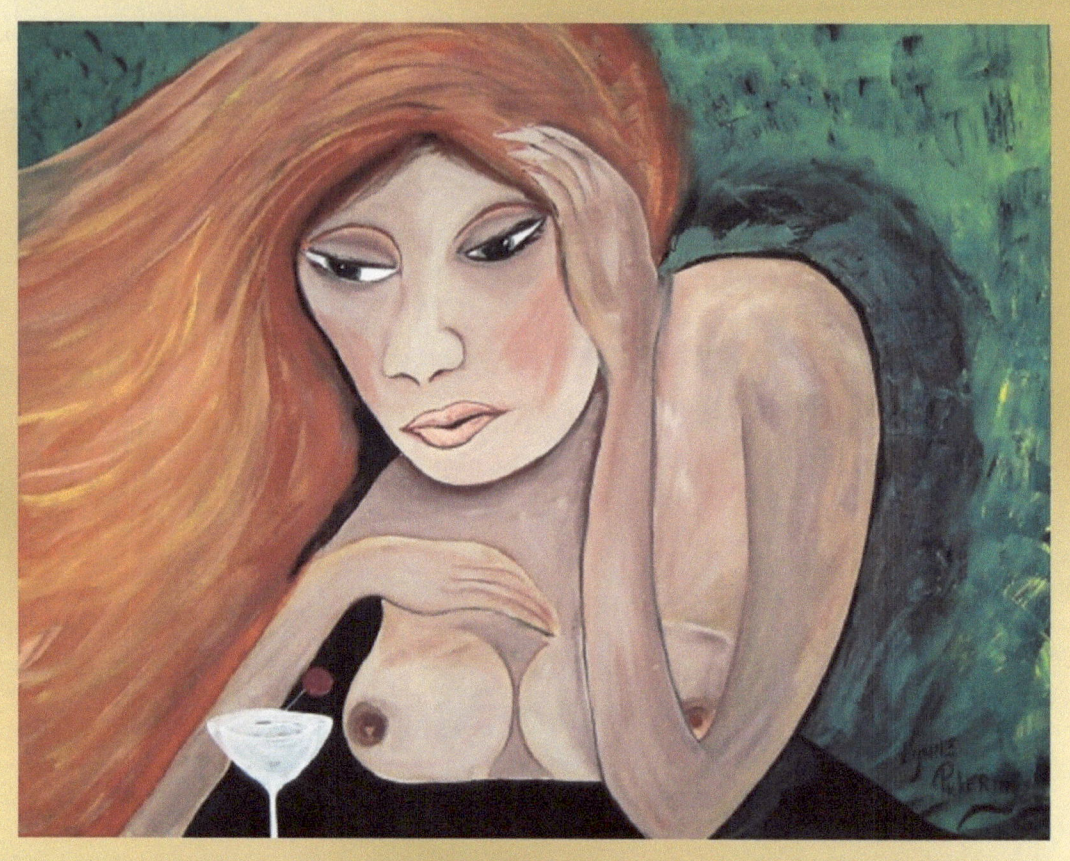

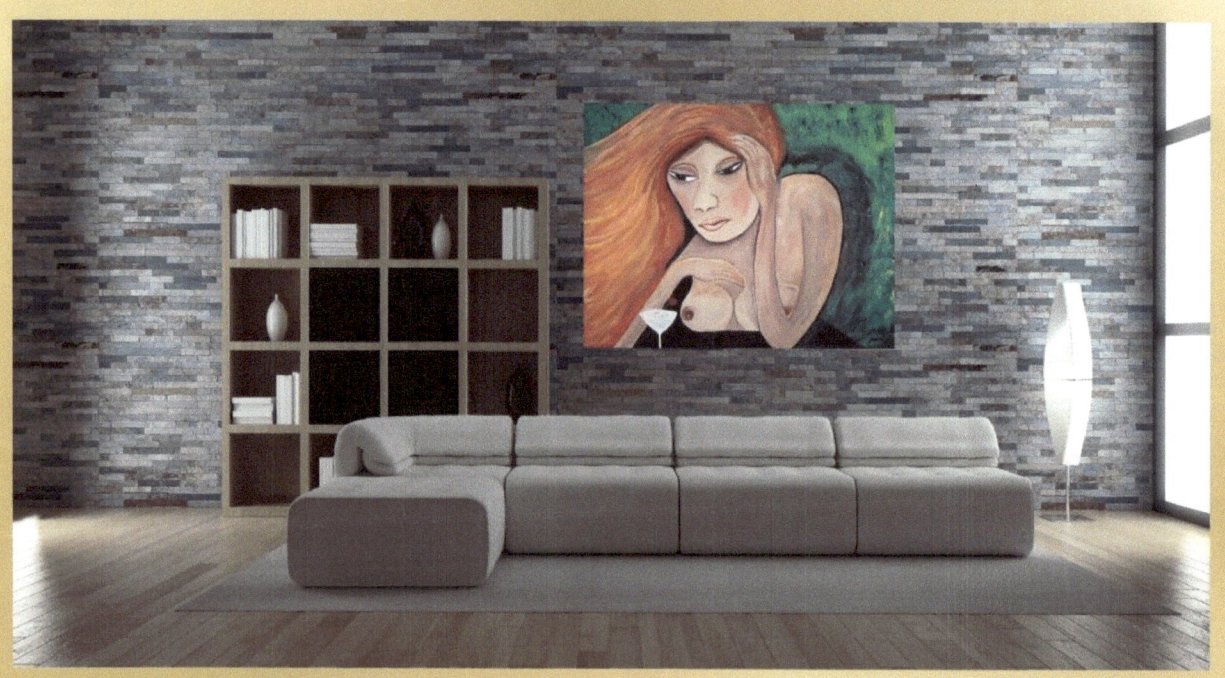

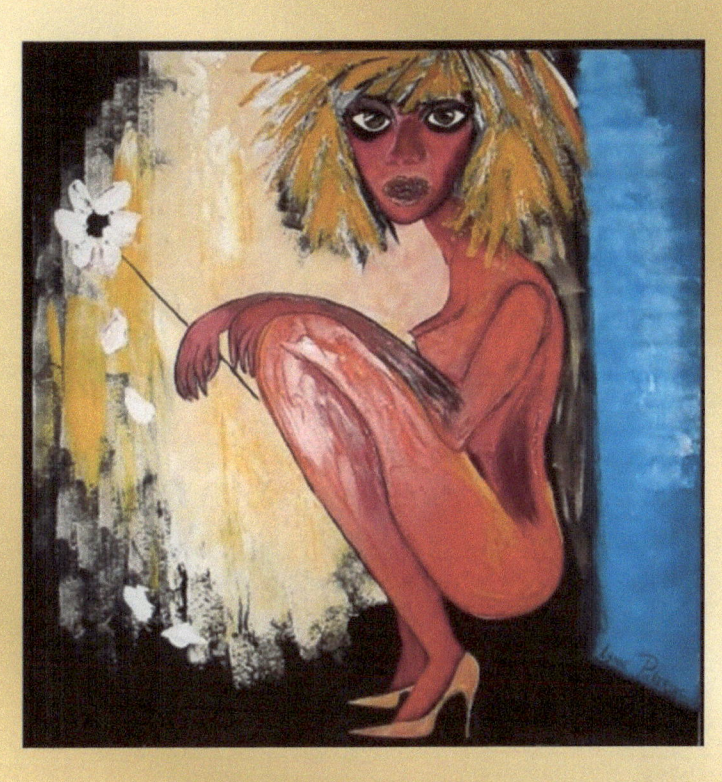

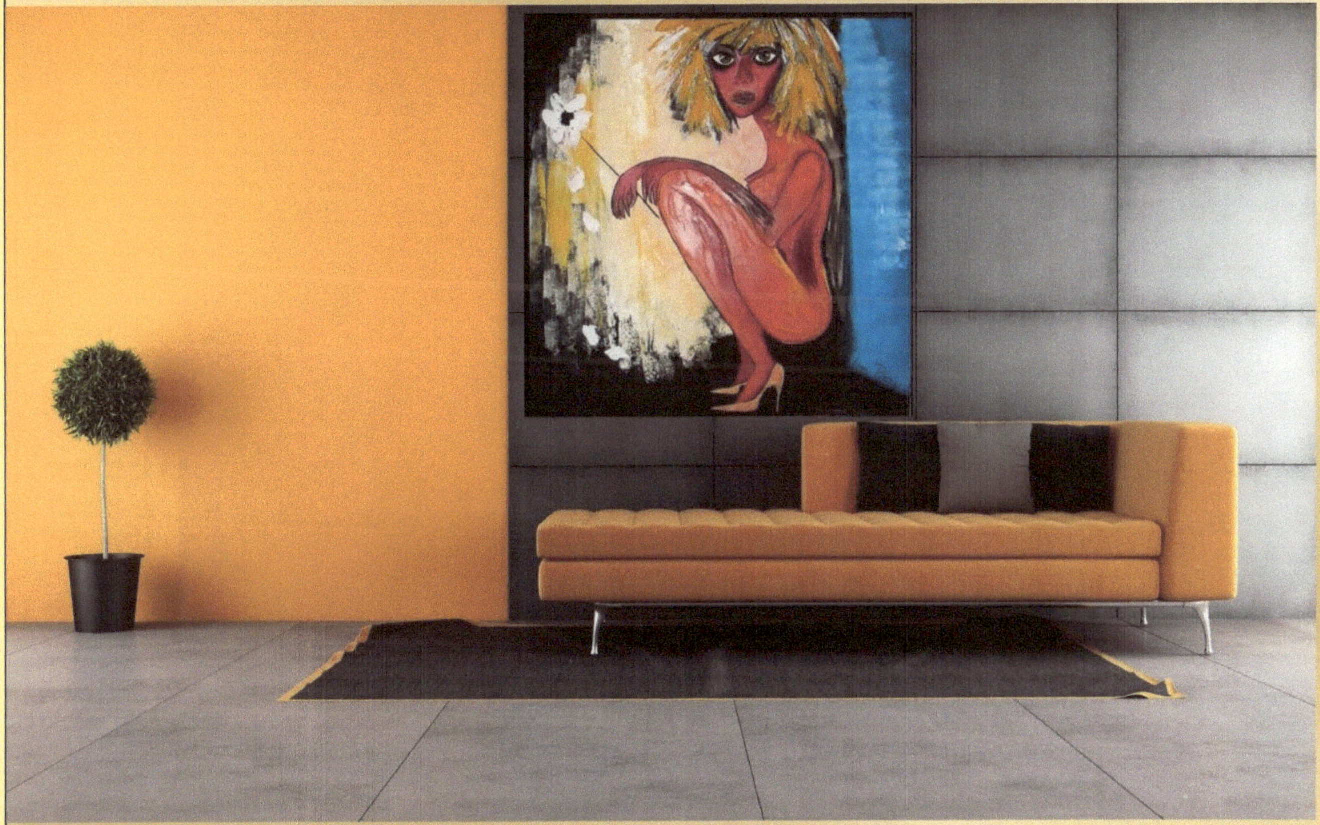

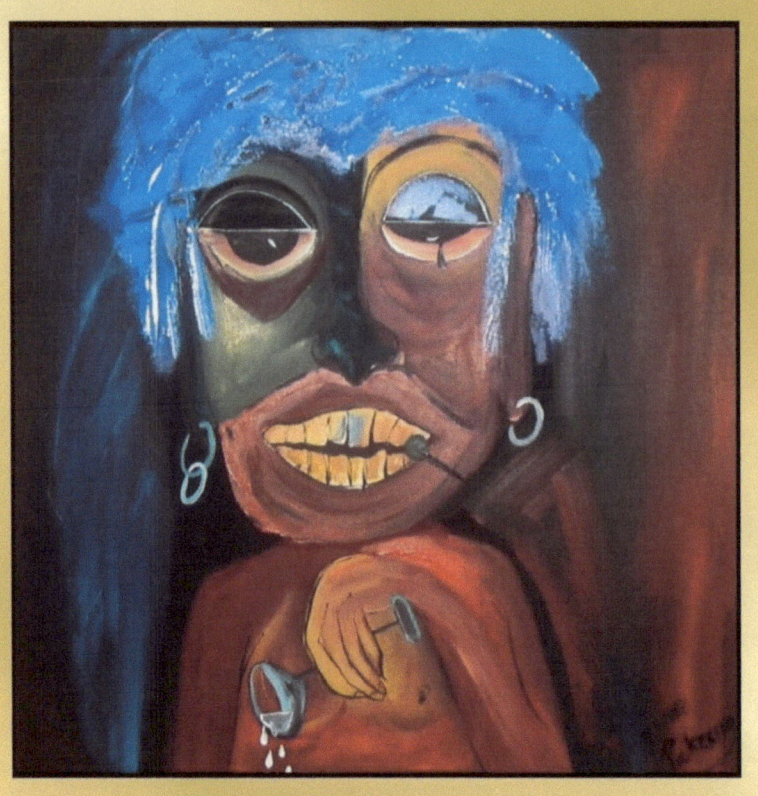

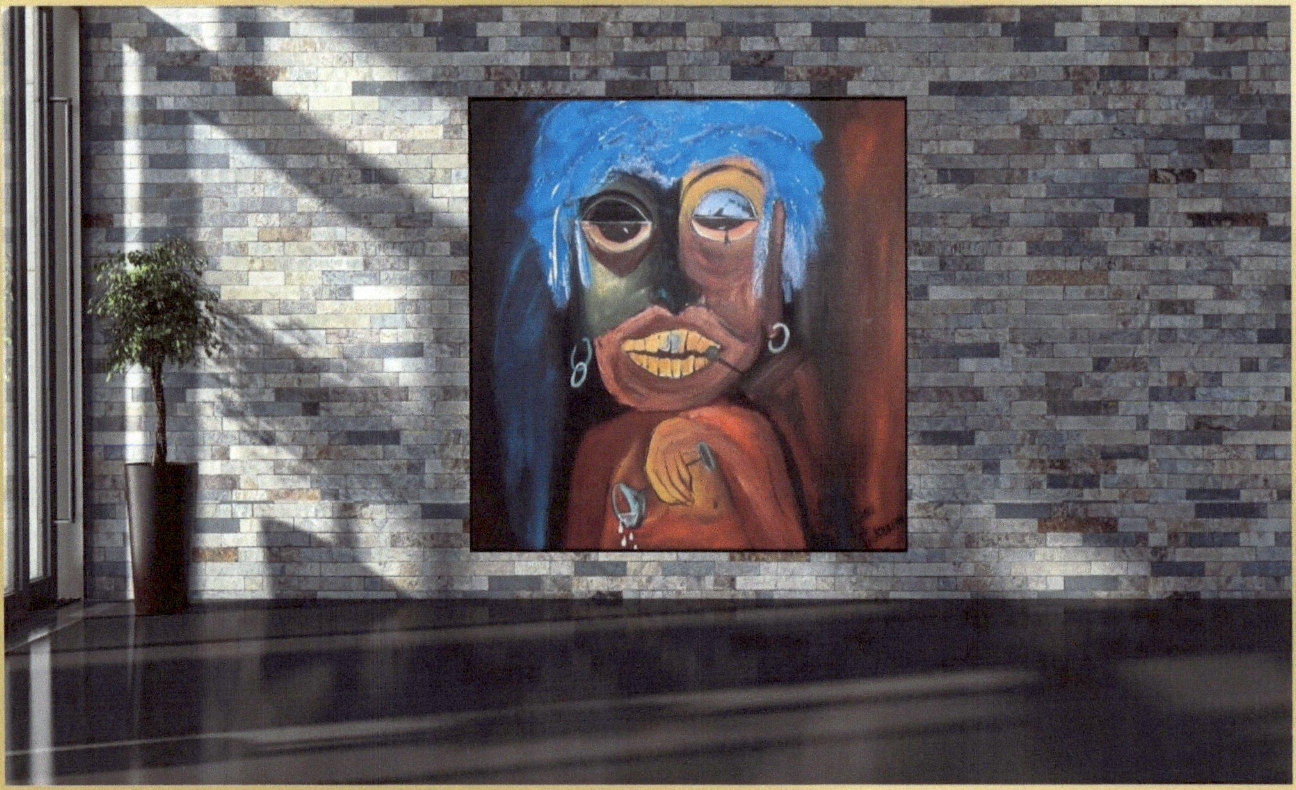

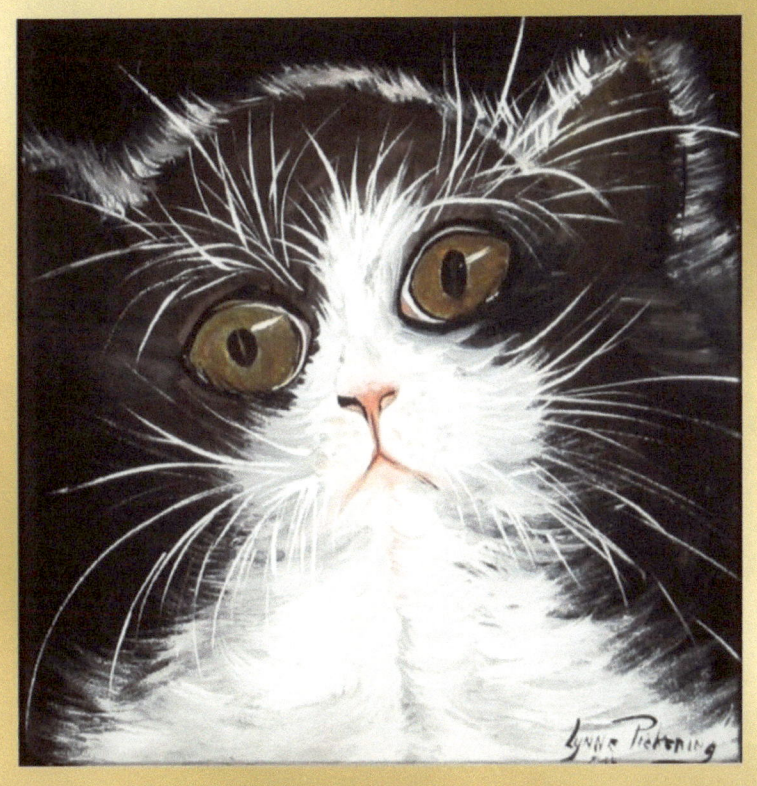

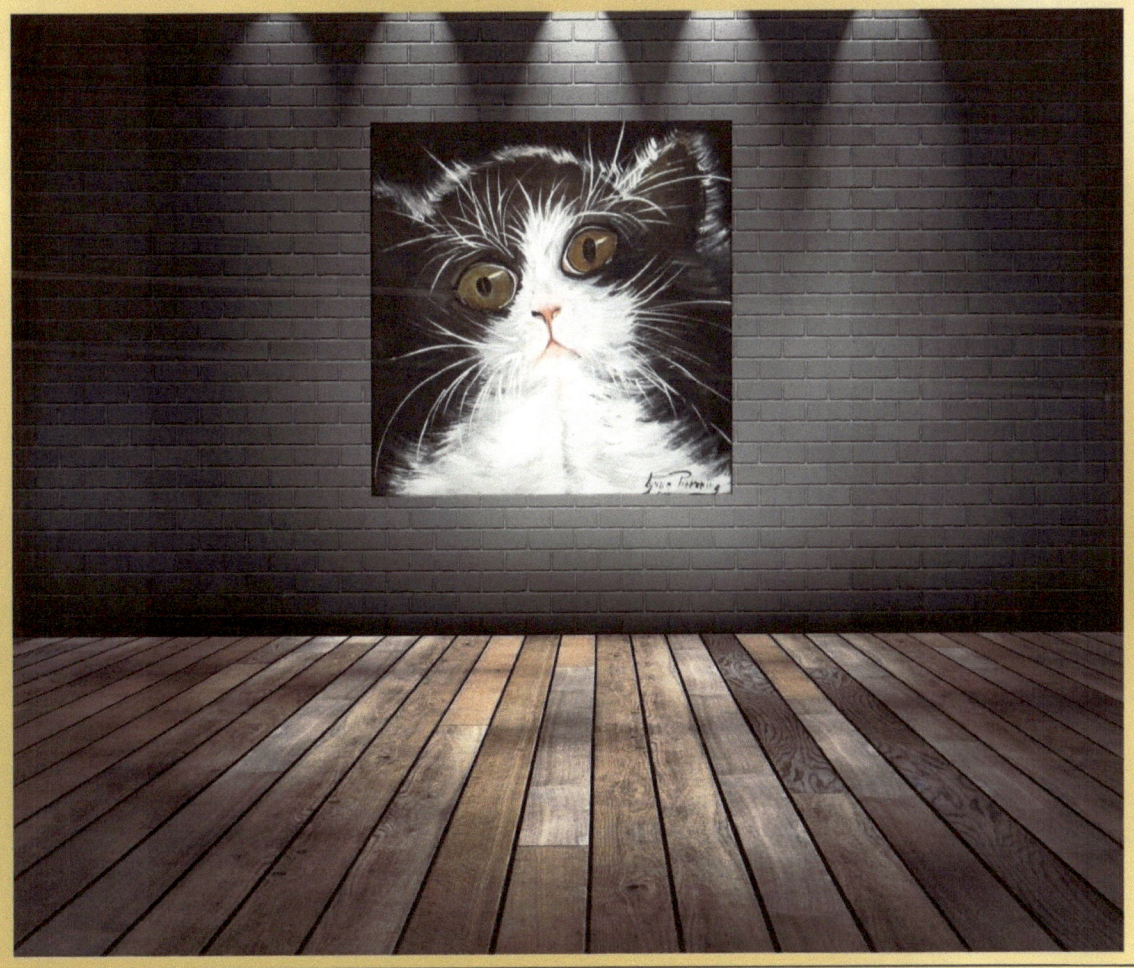

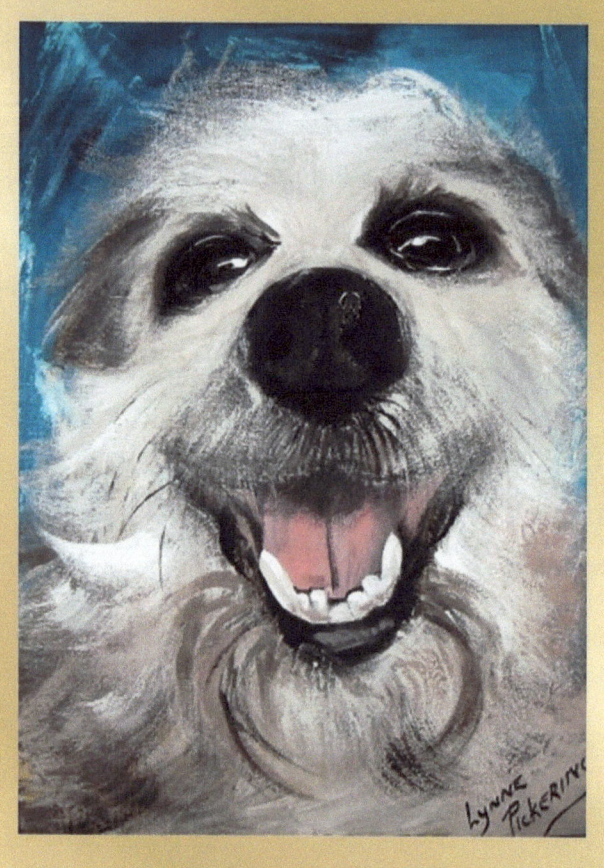

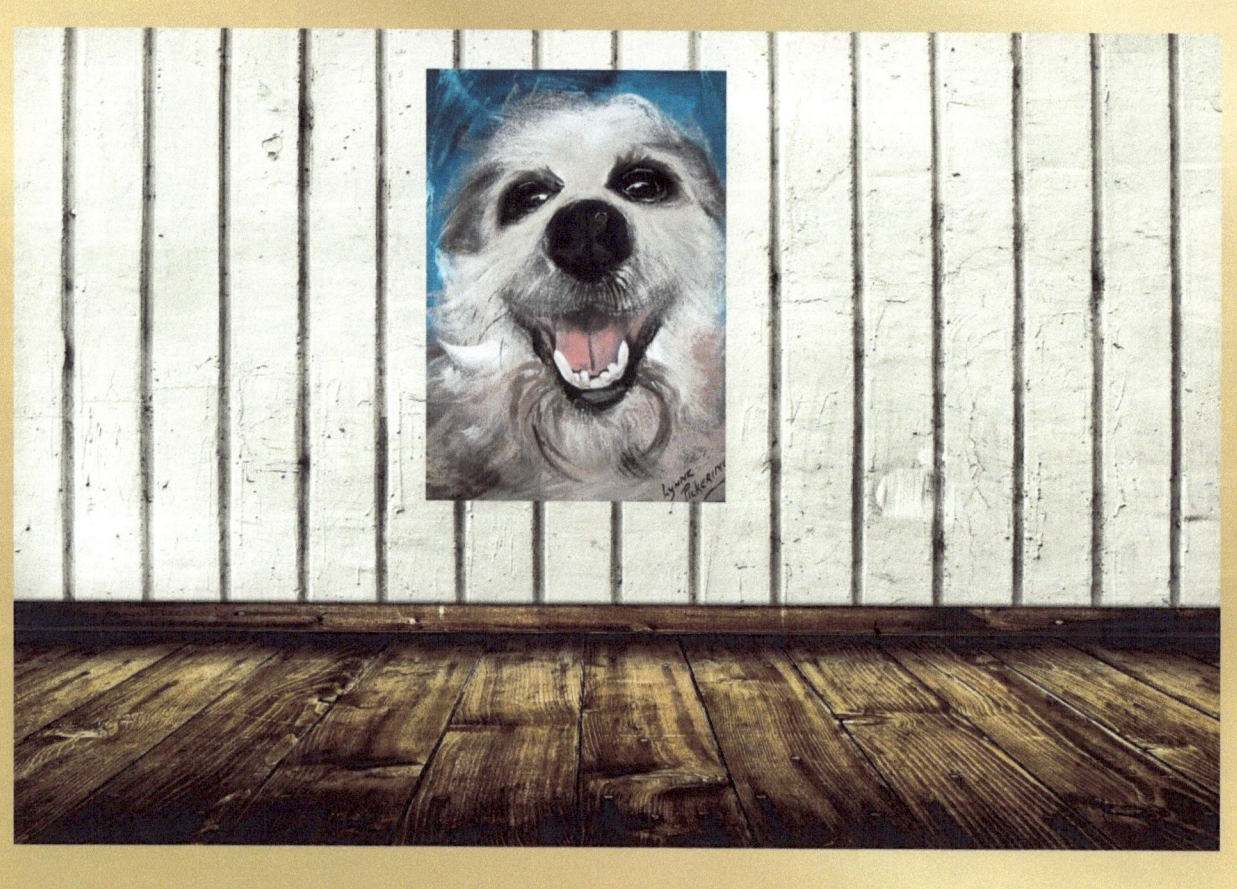

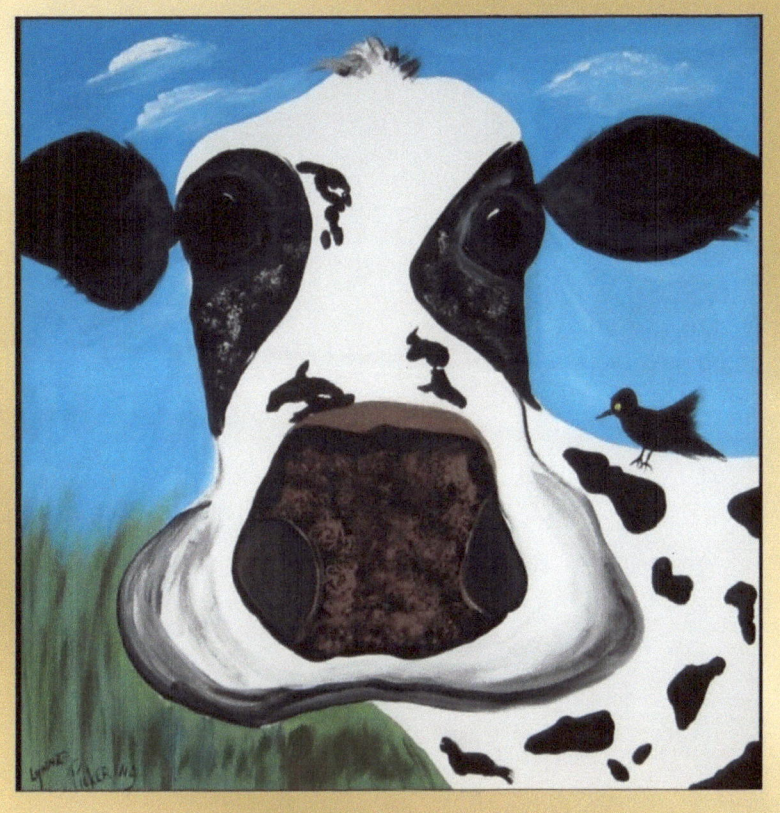

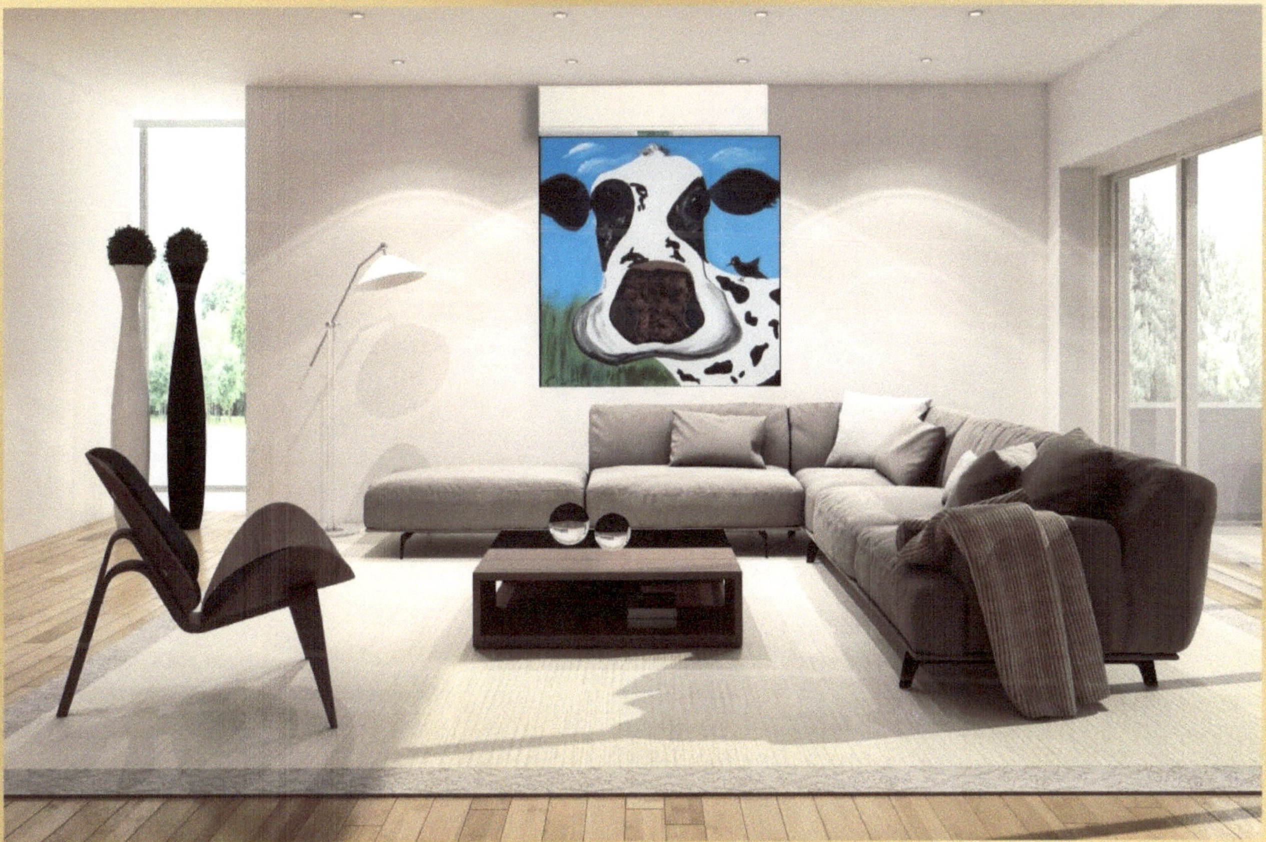

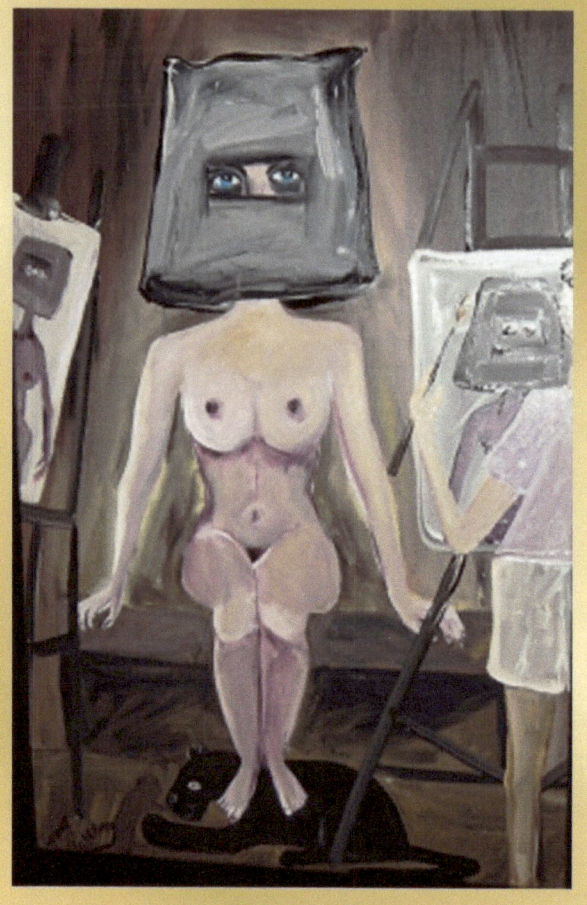

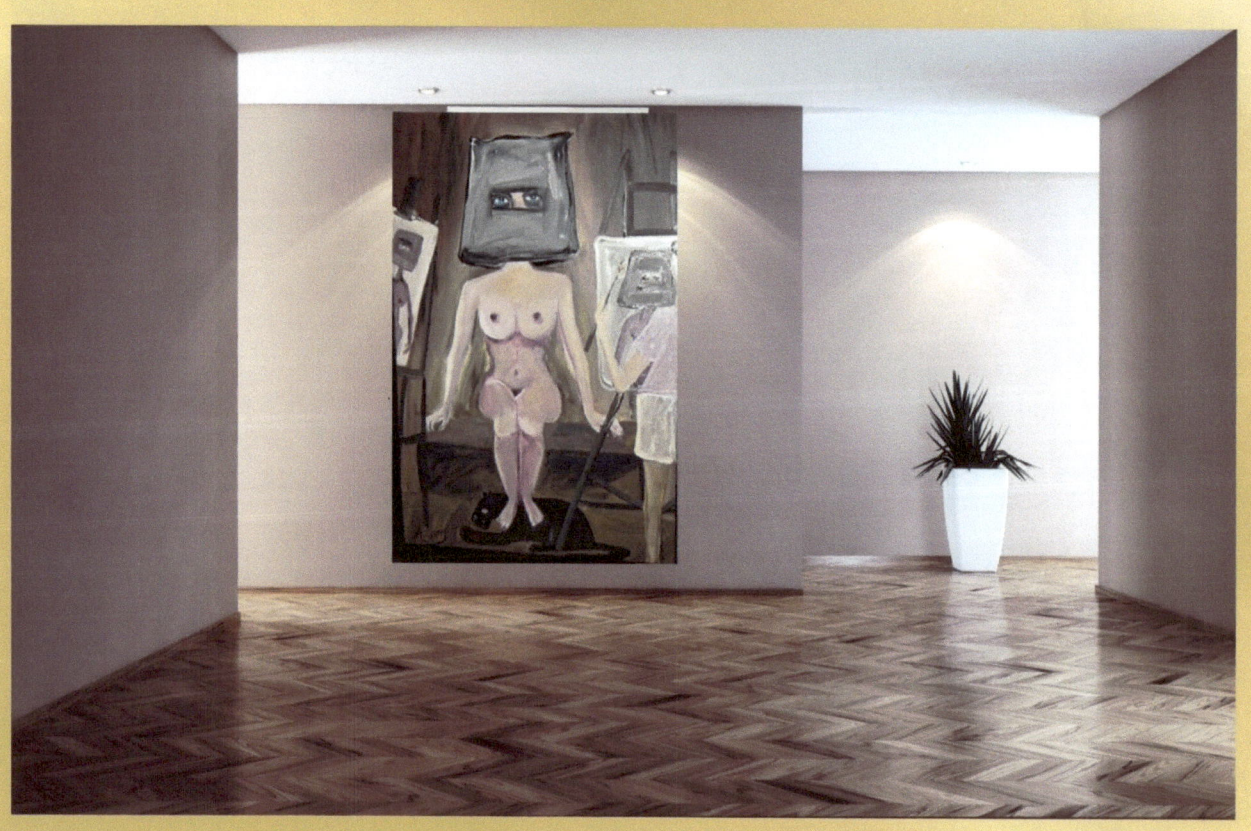

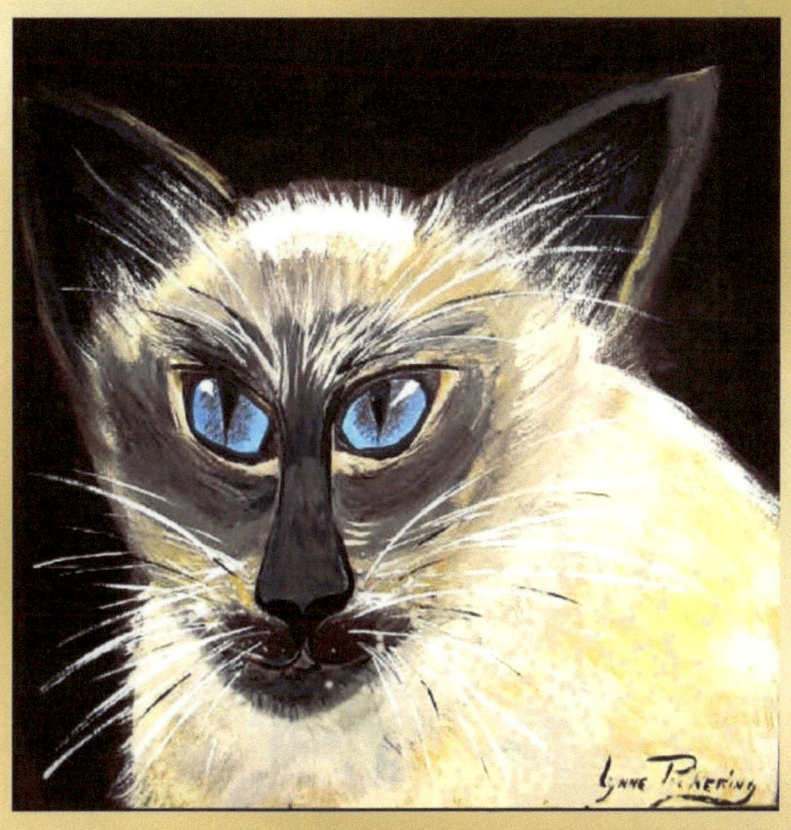

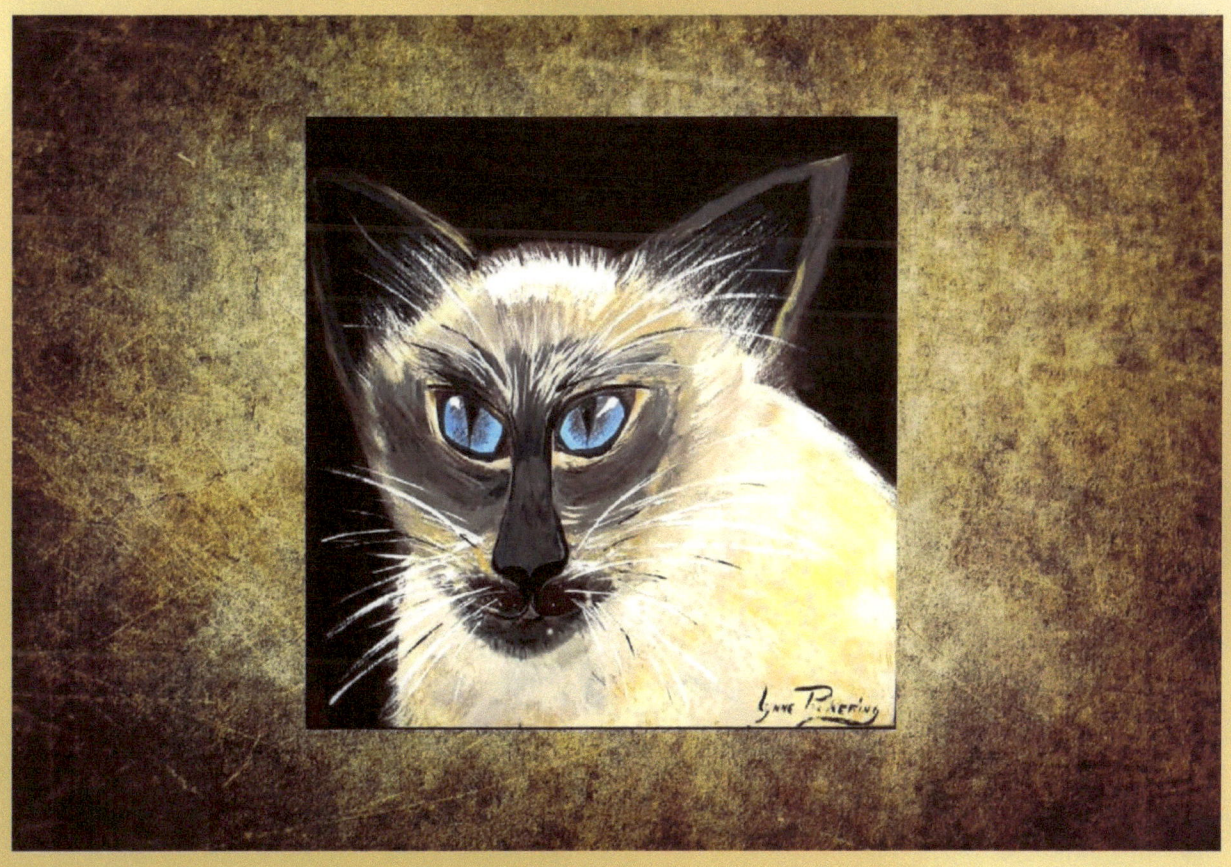

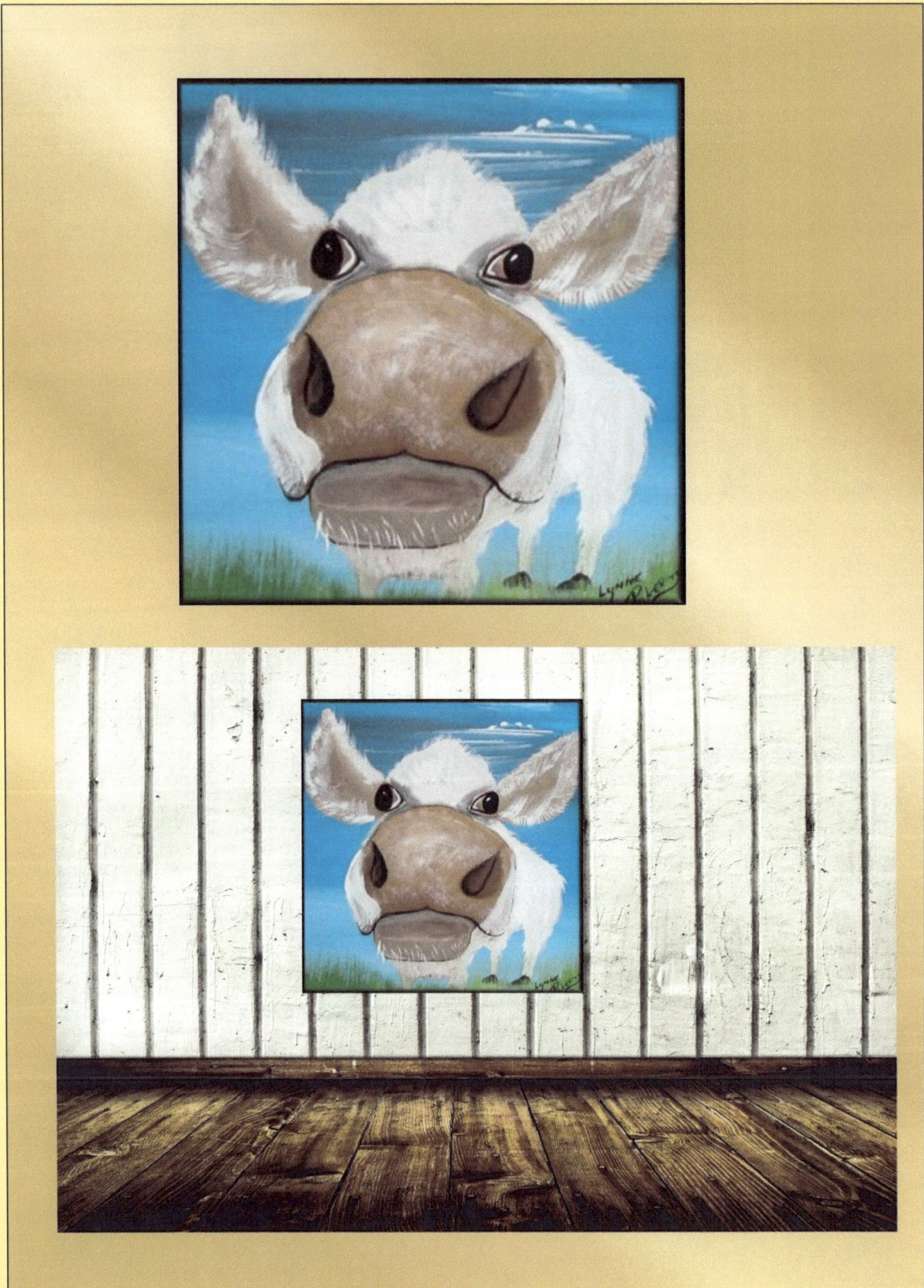

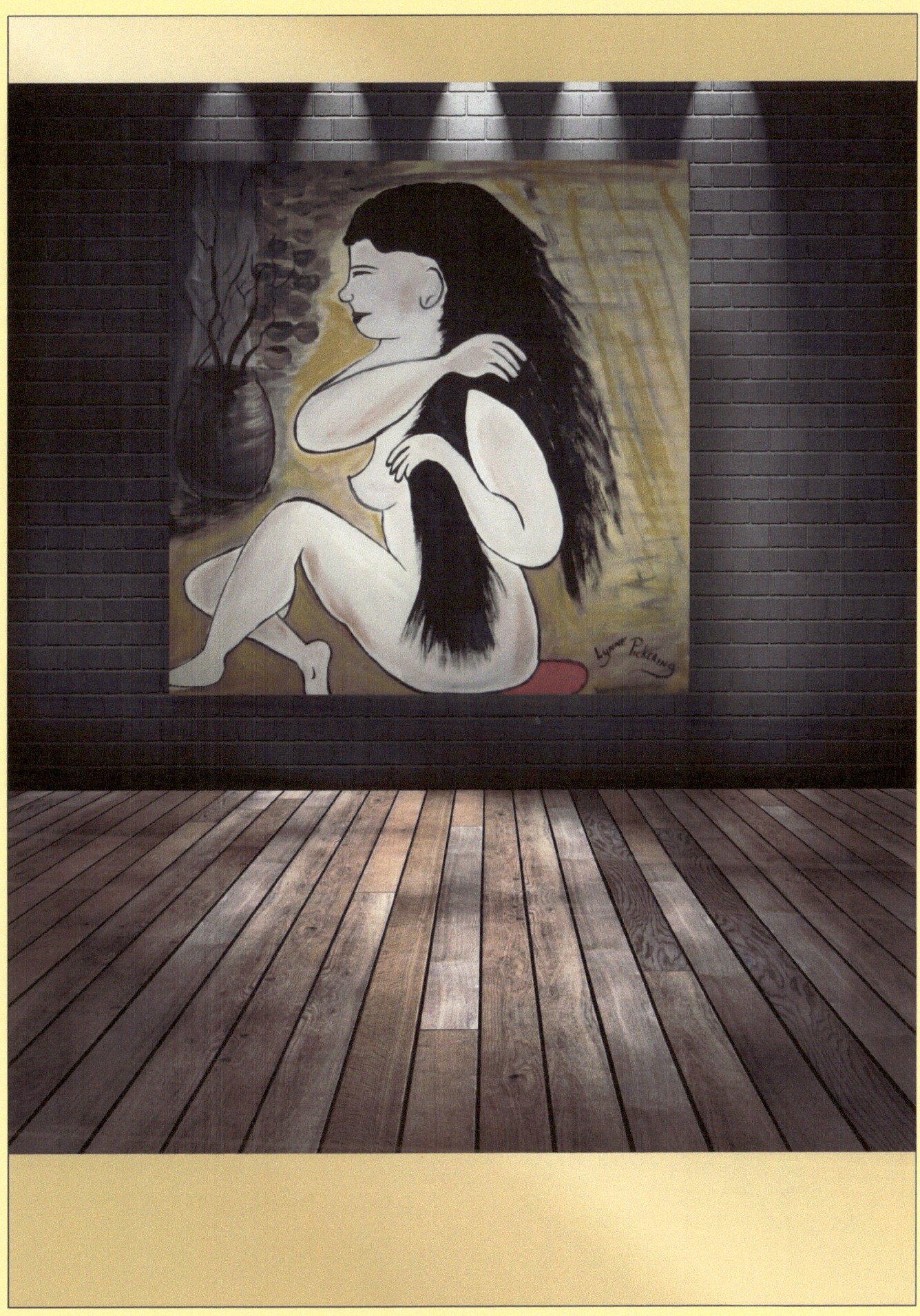

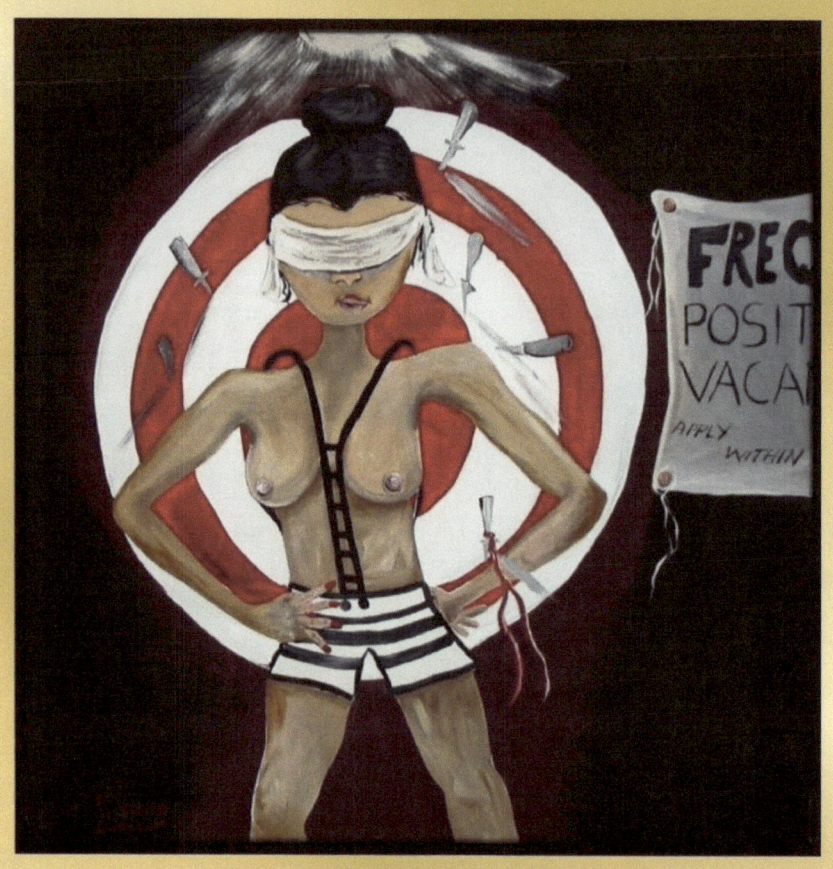

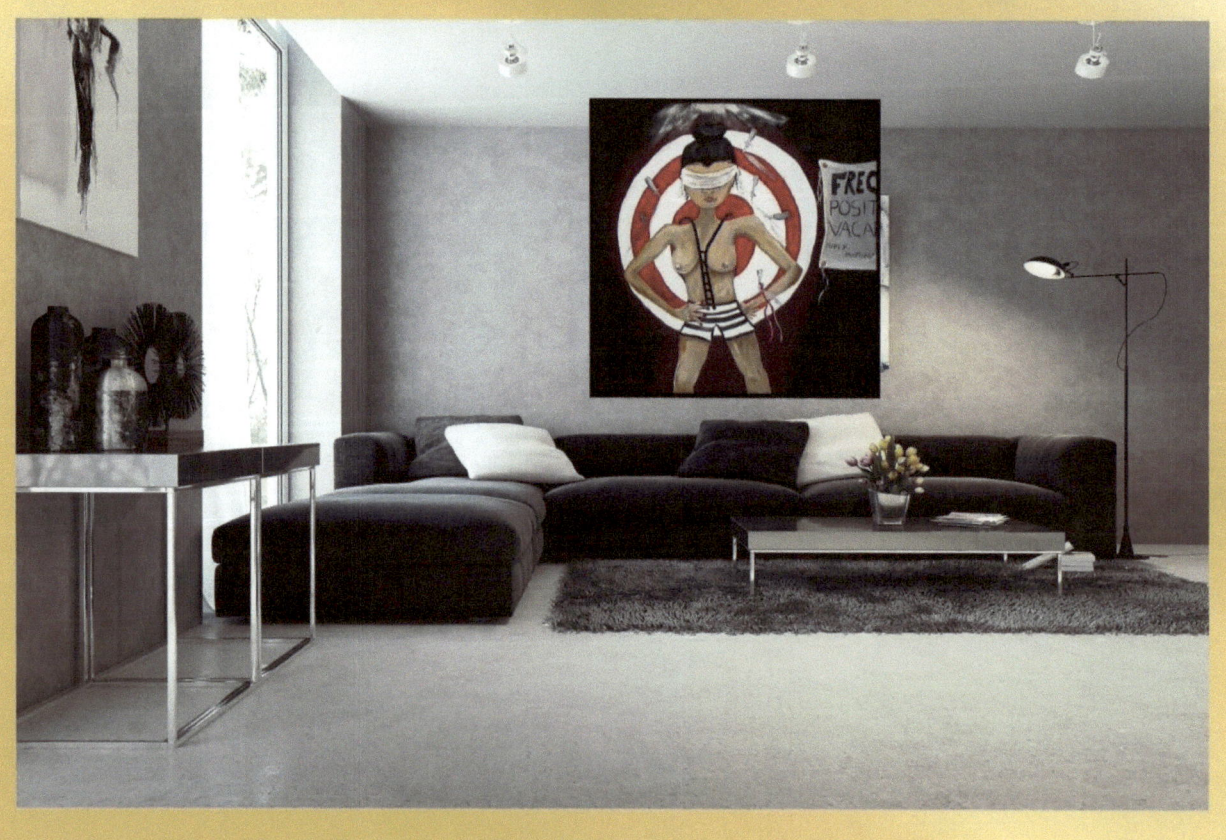

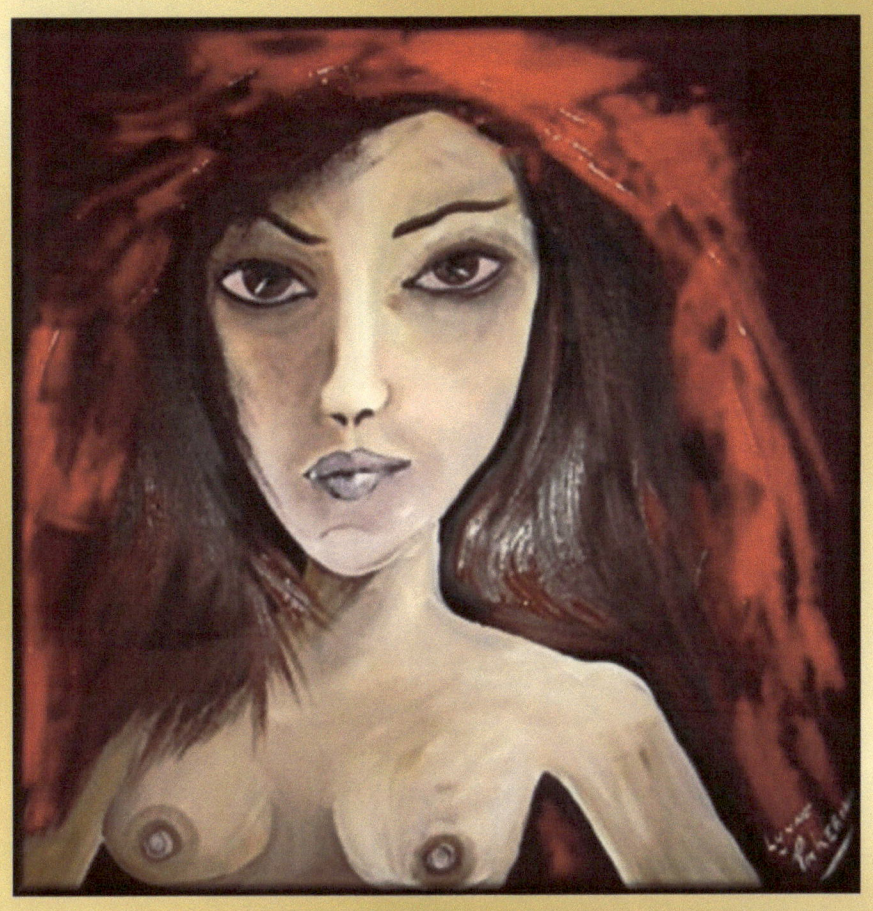

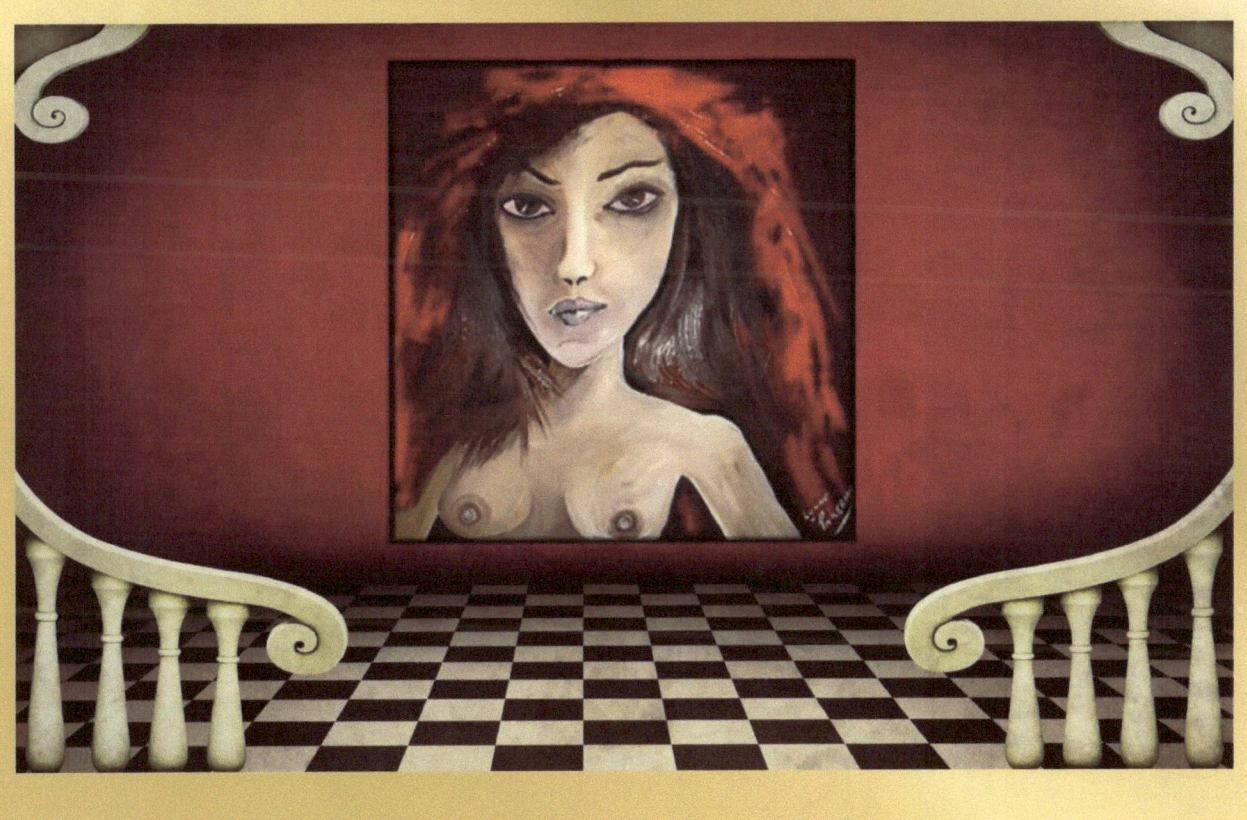

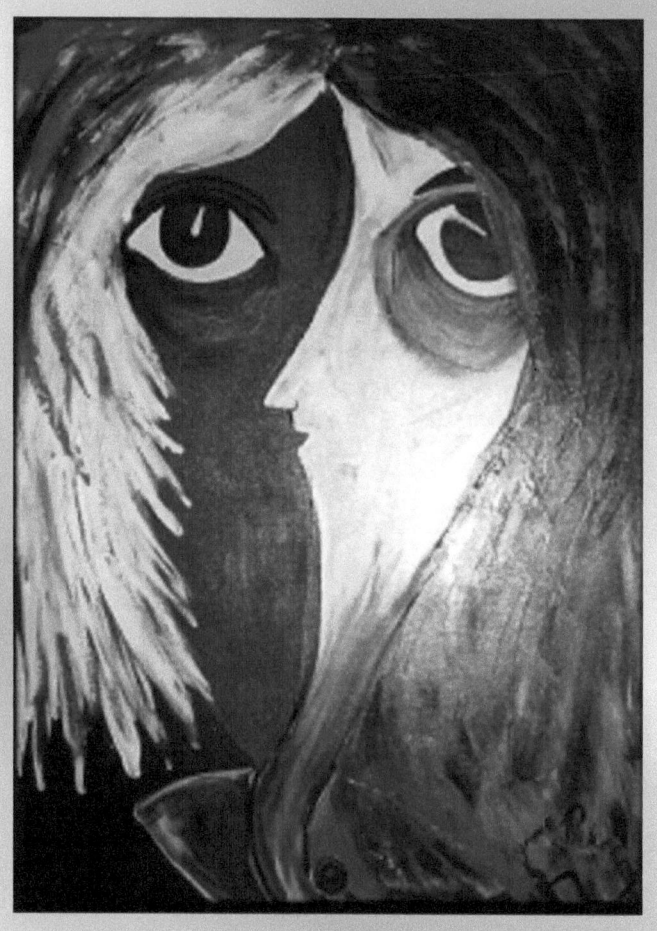

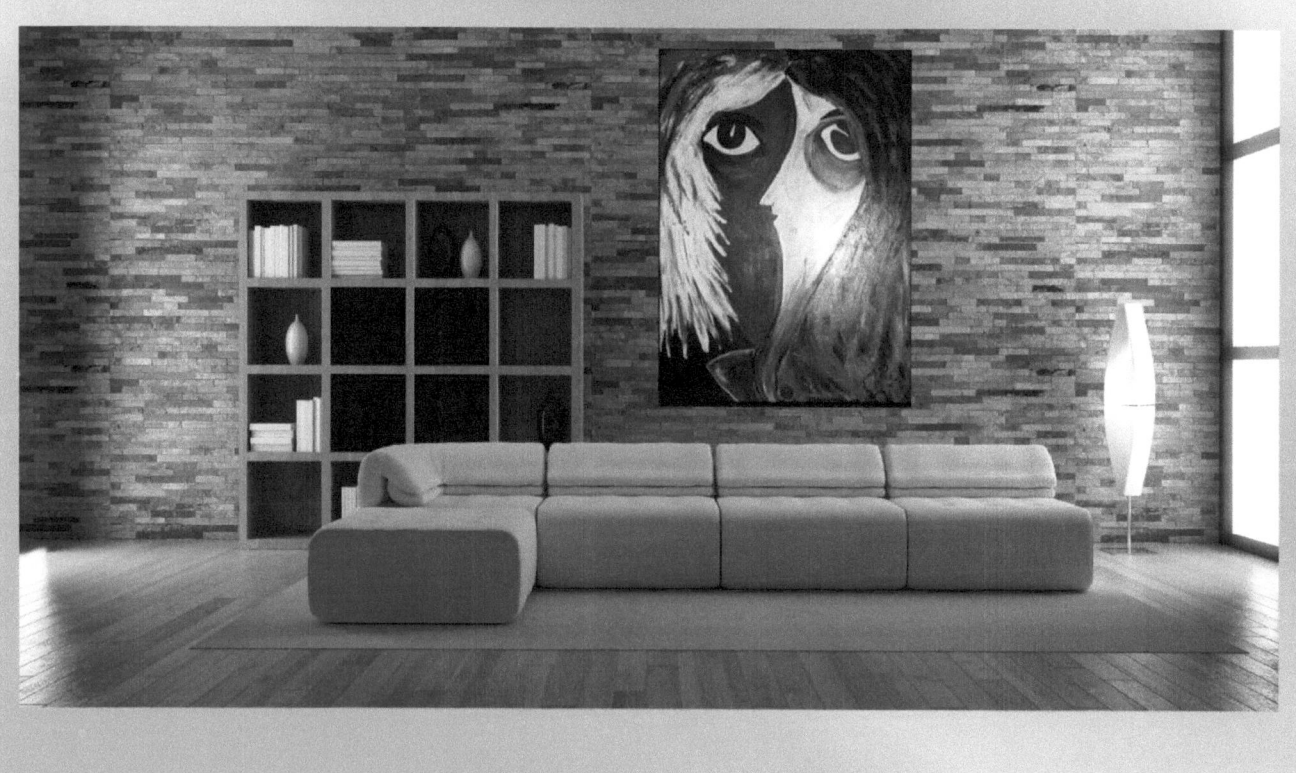

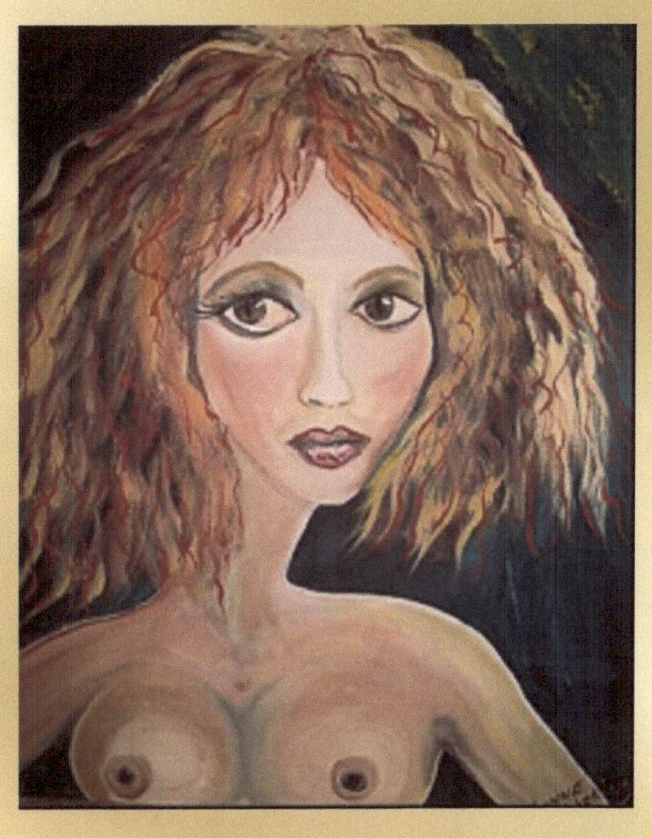

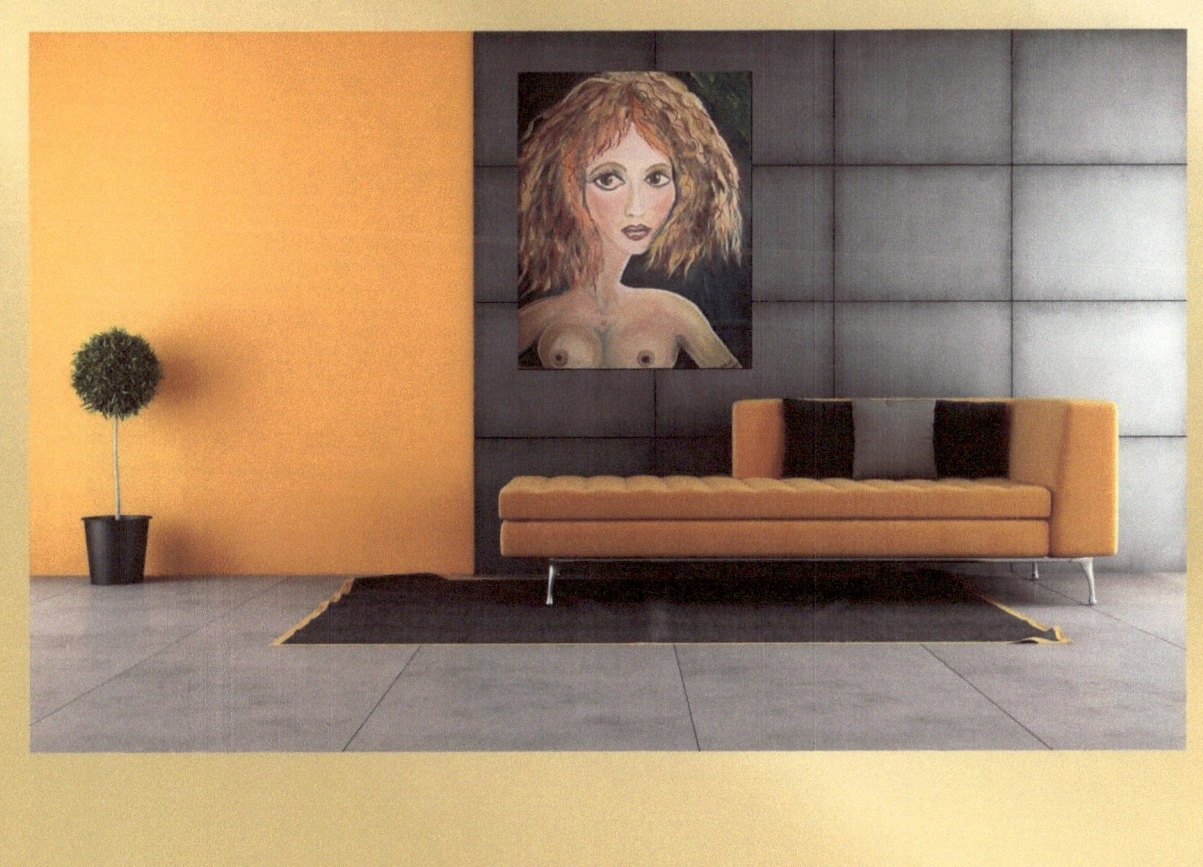

35

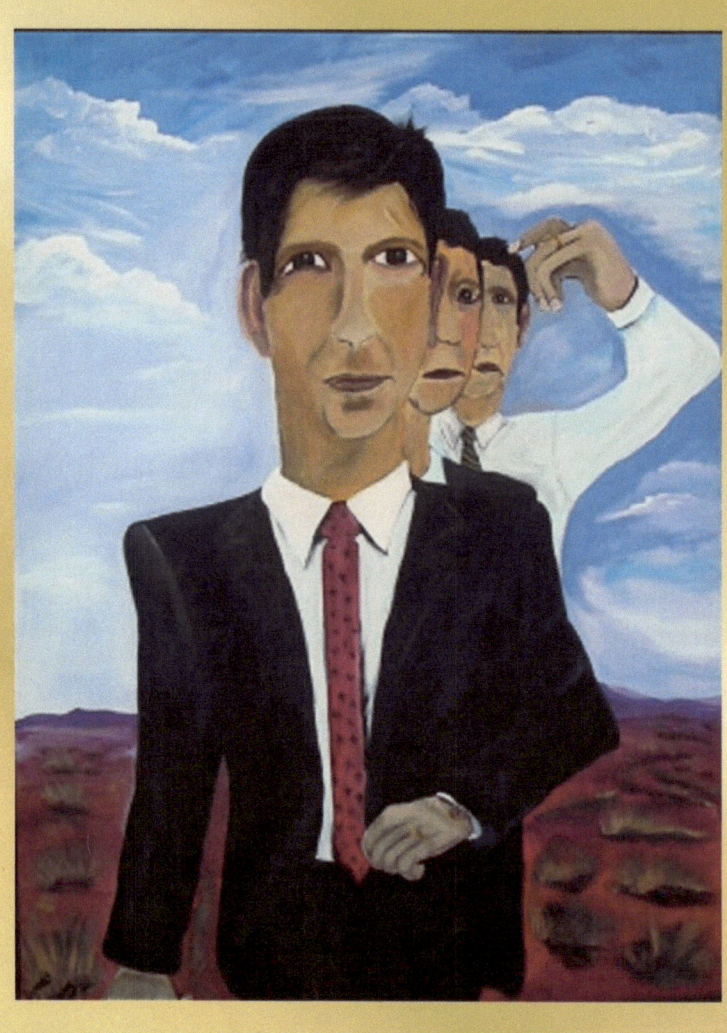

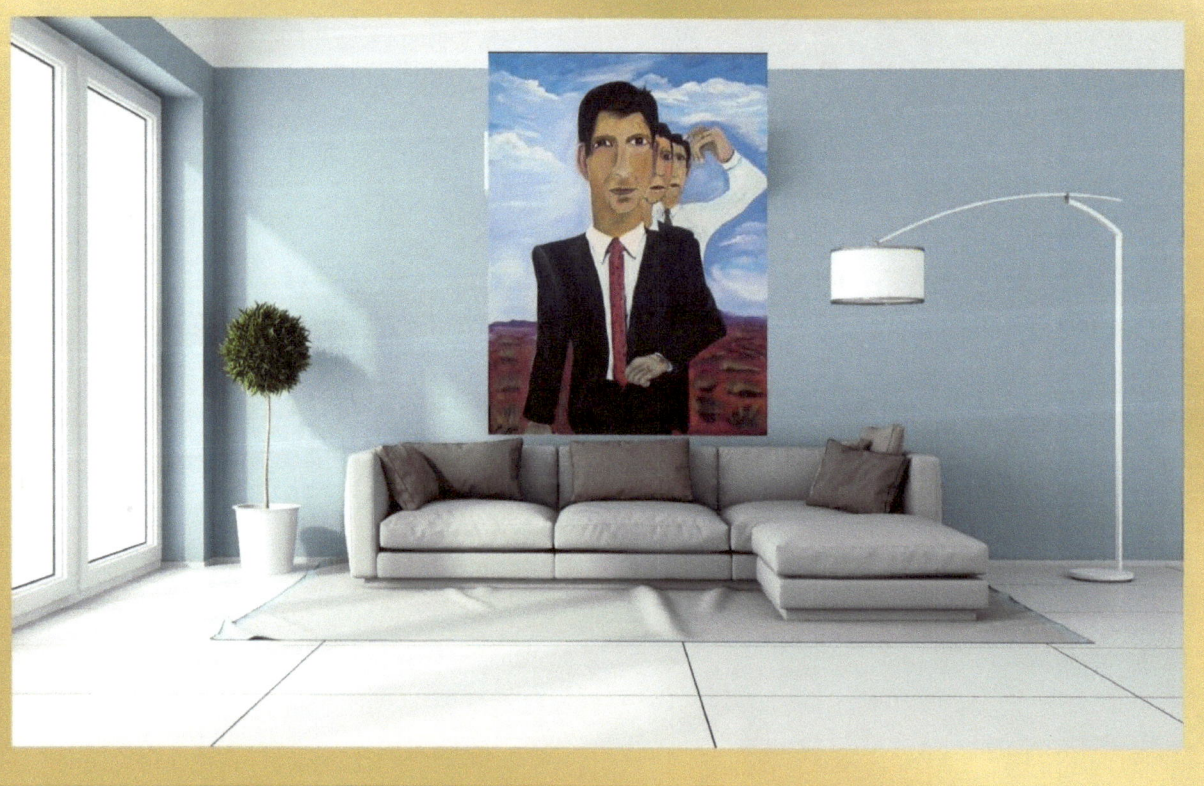

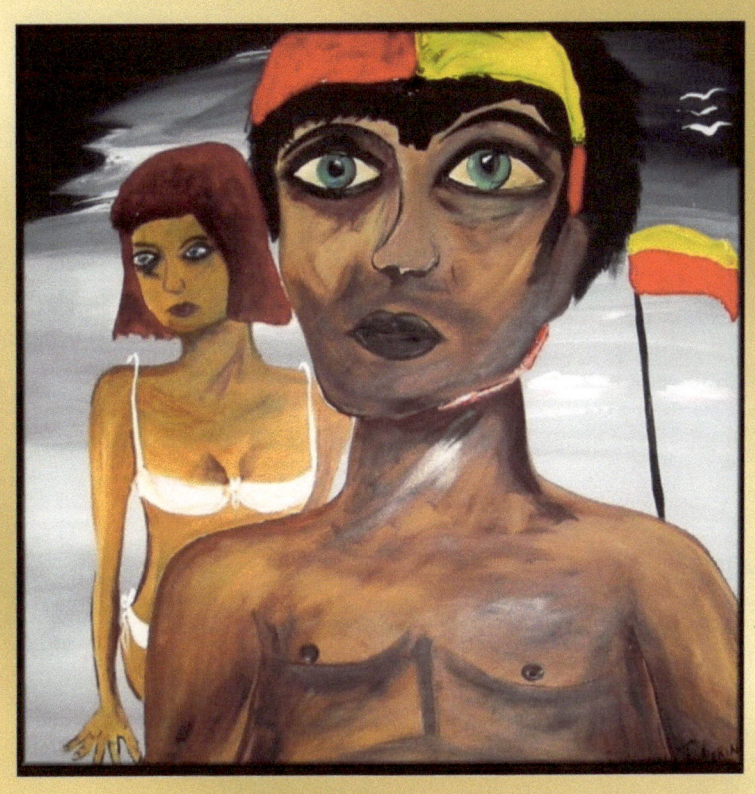

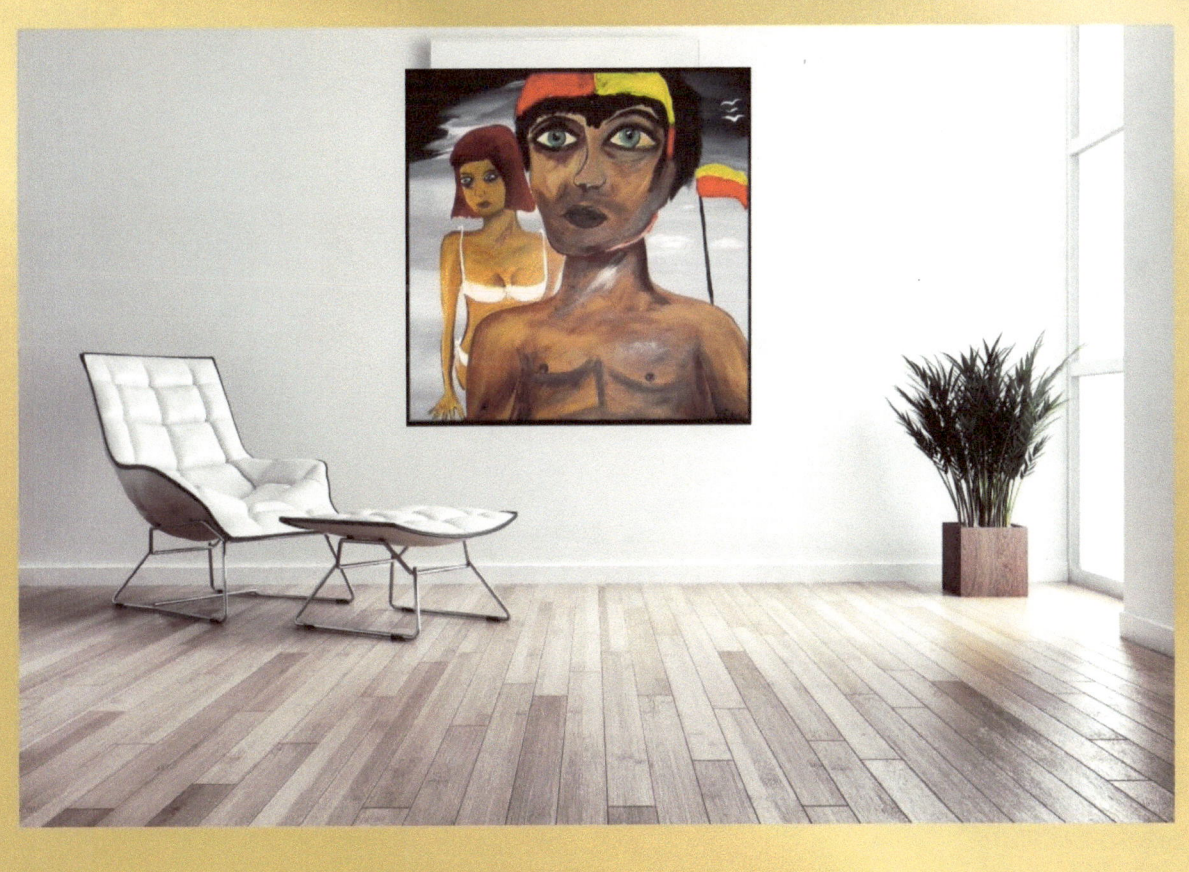

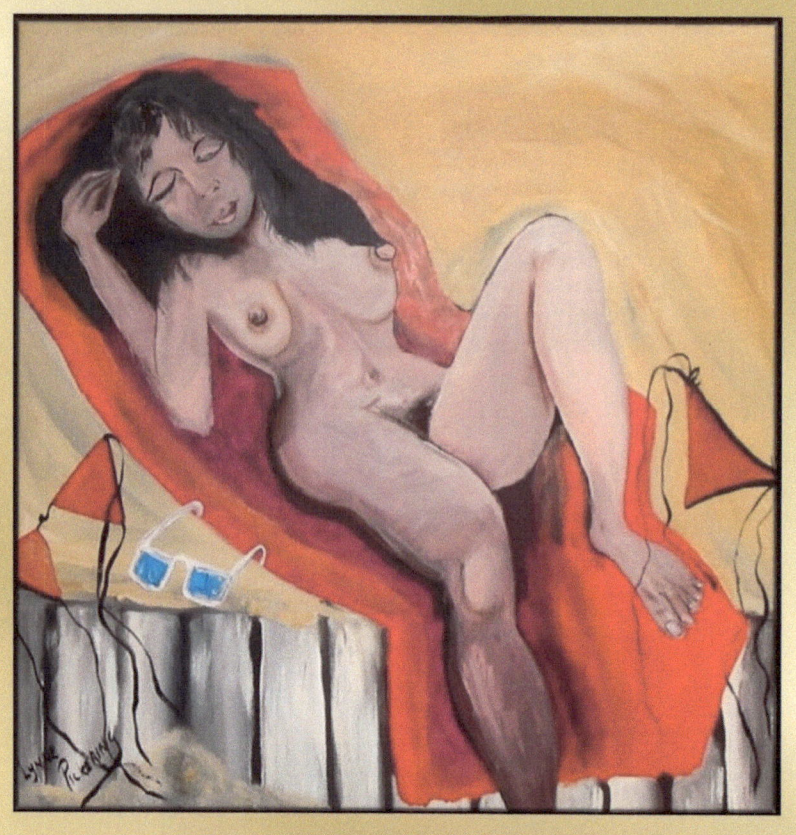

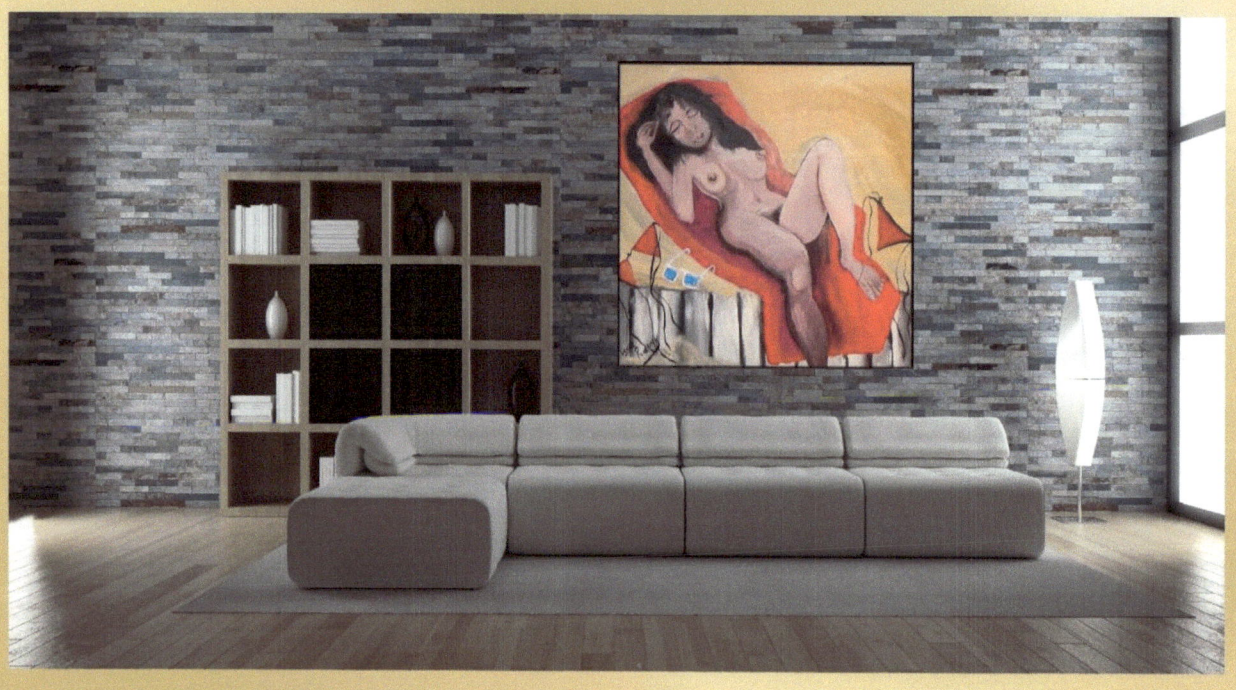

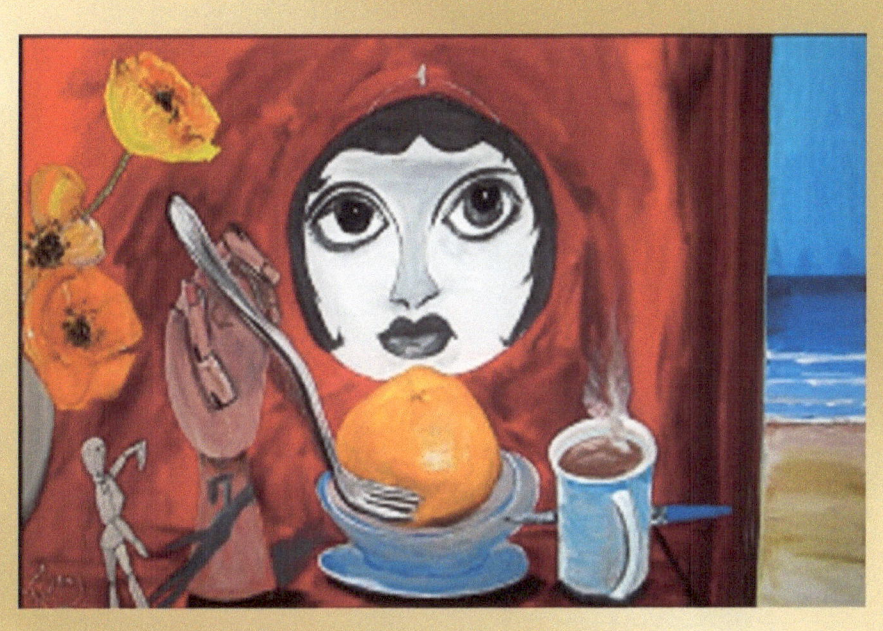

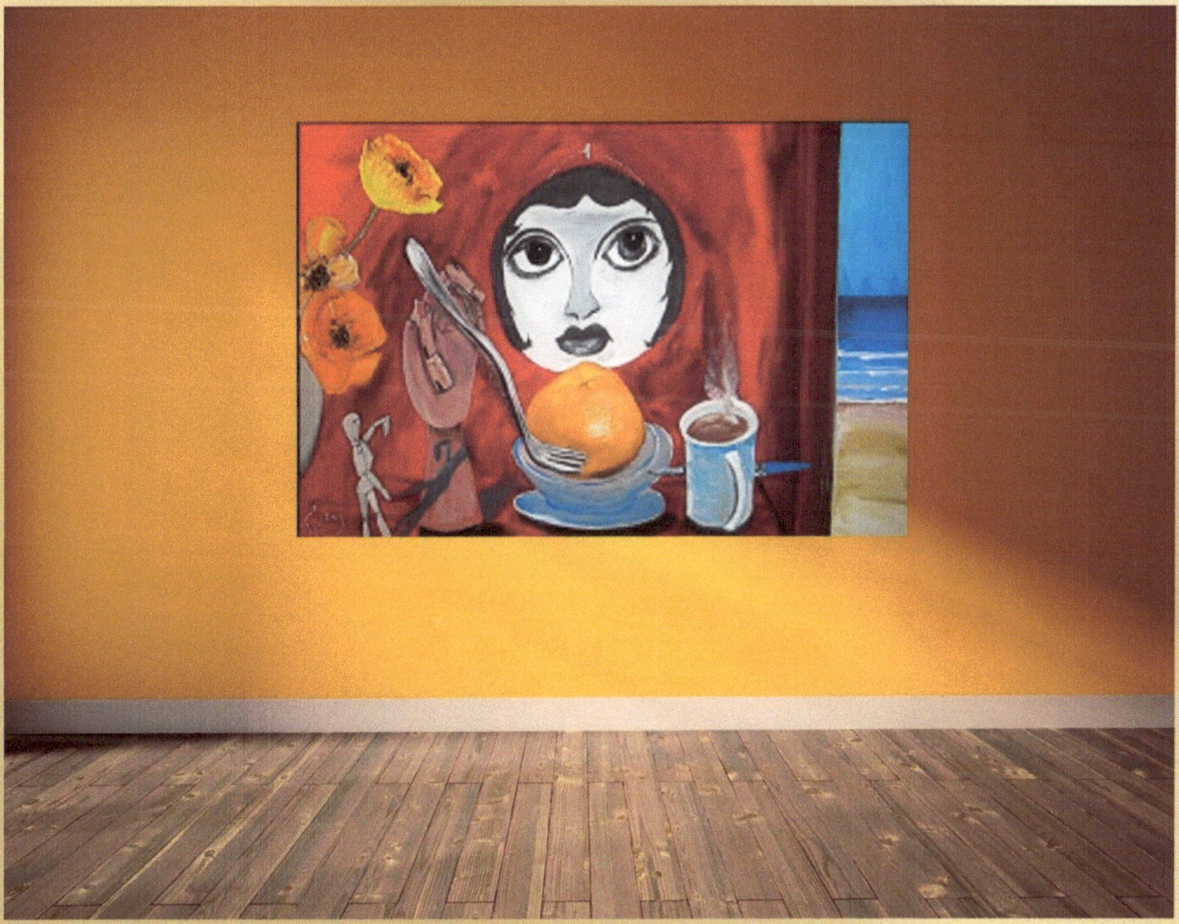

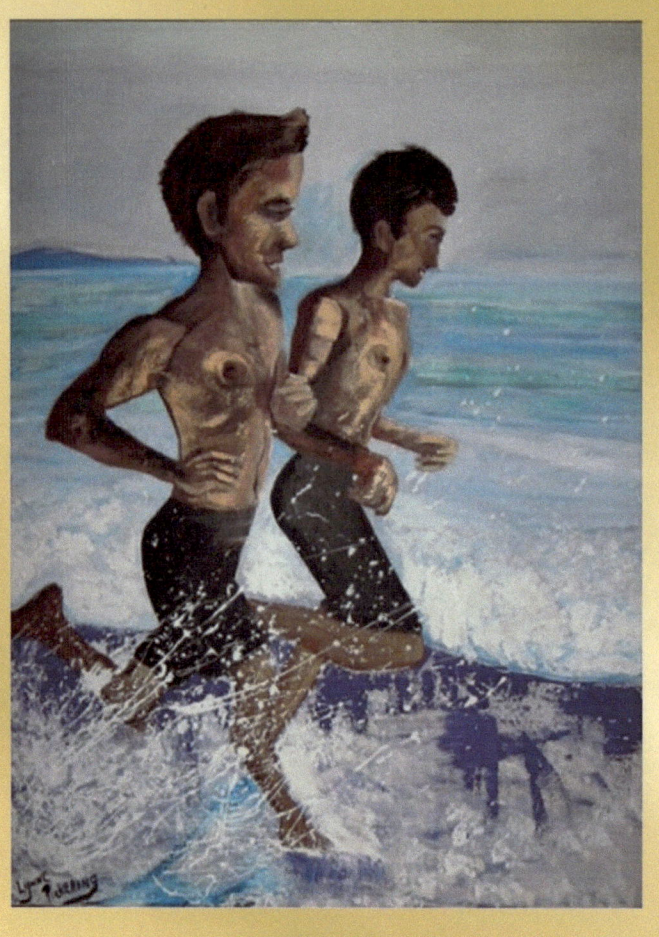

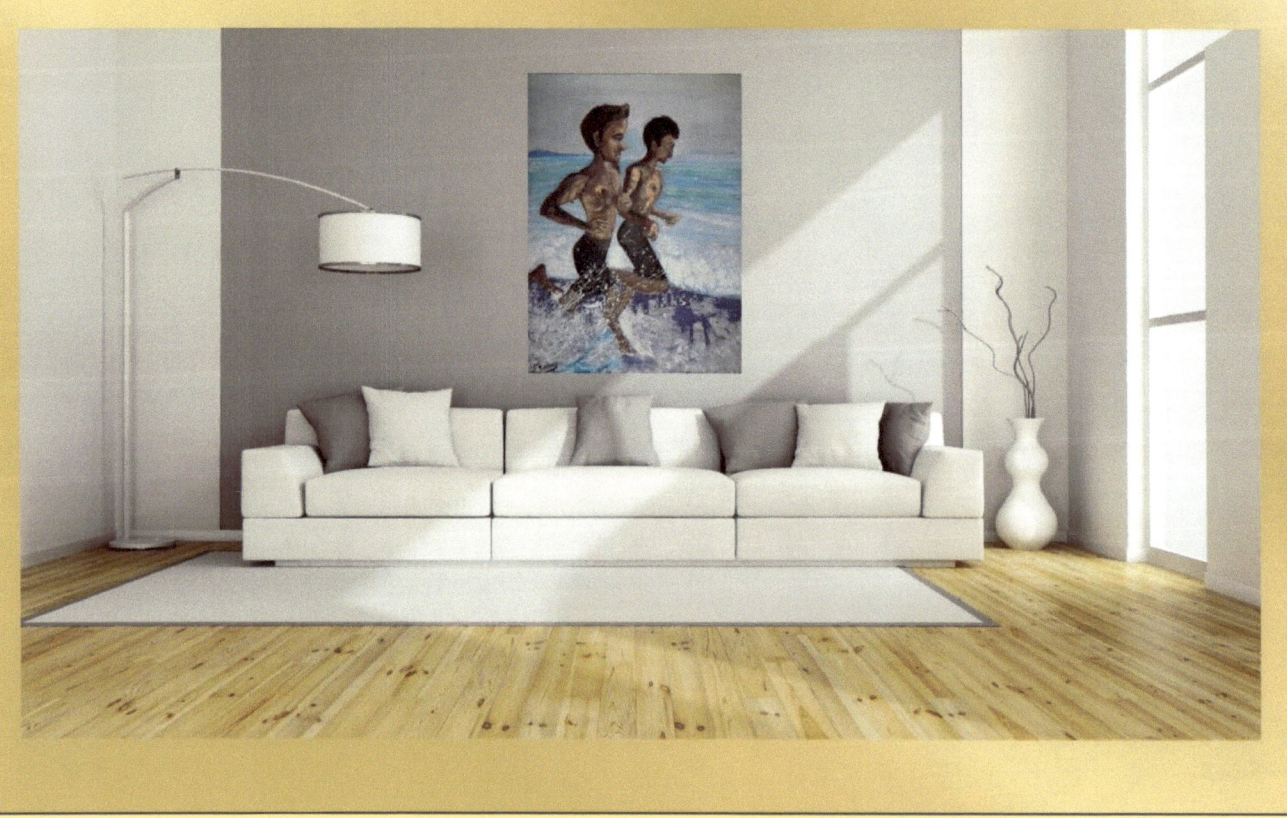

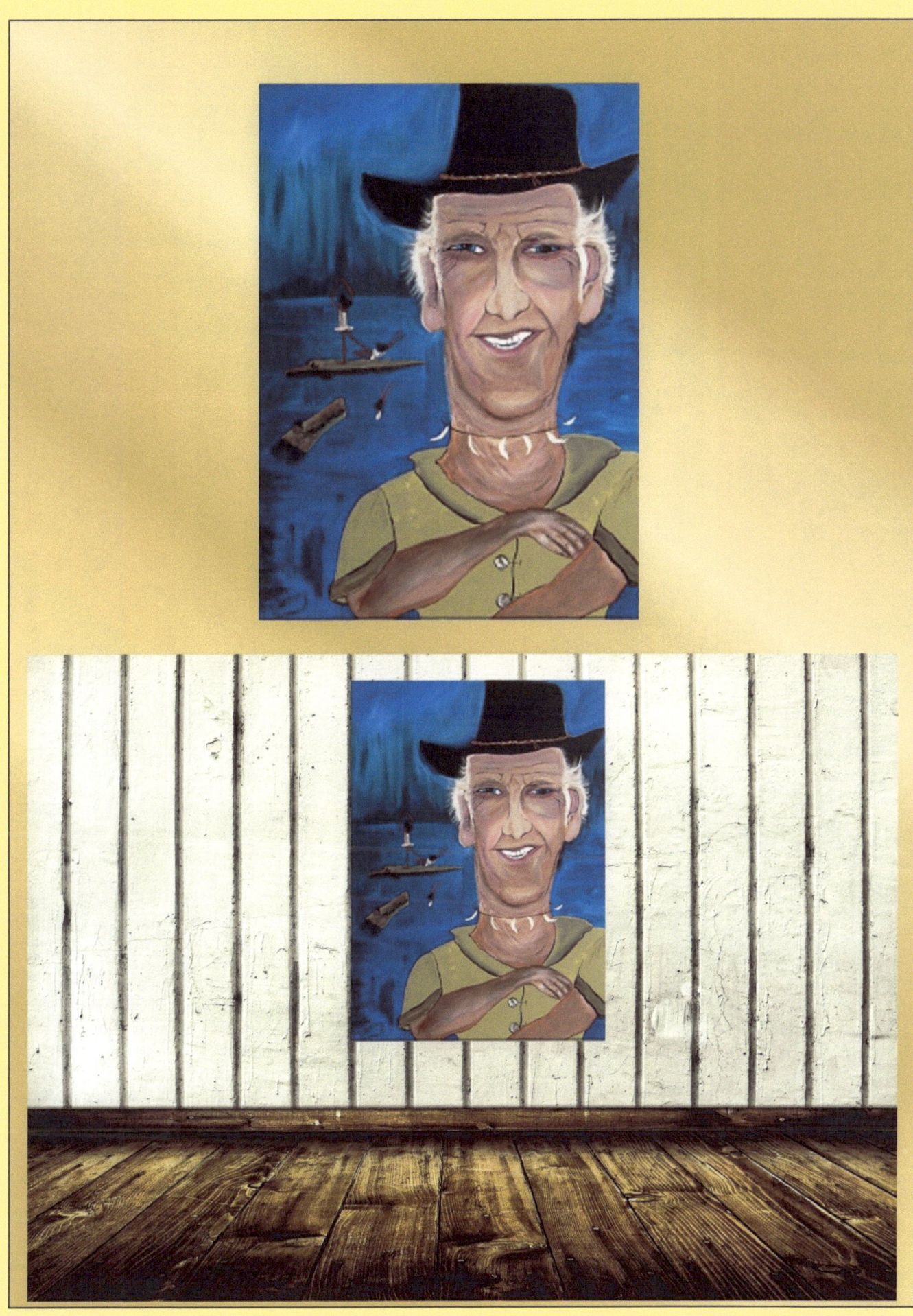

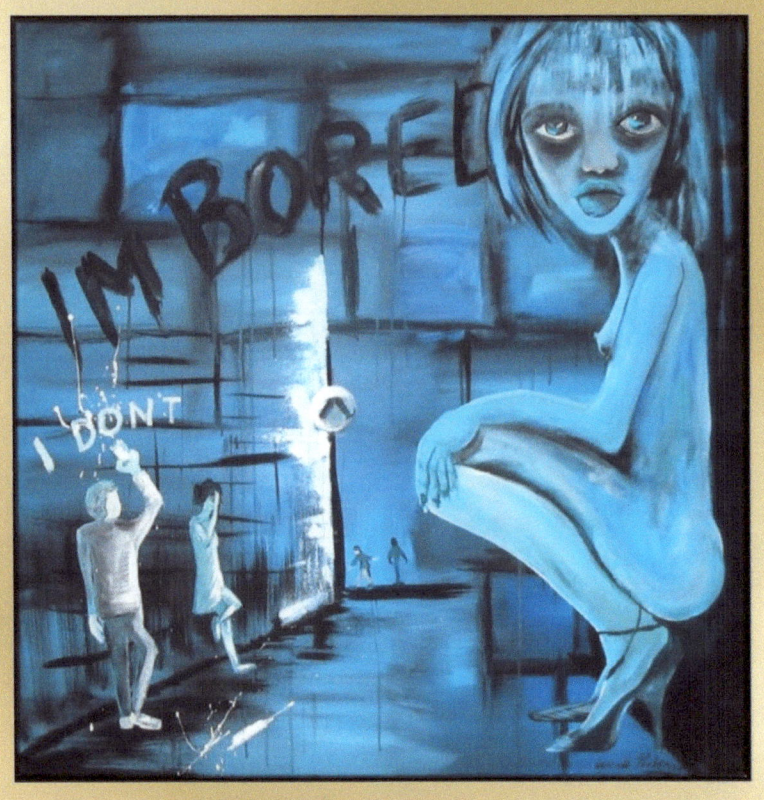

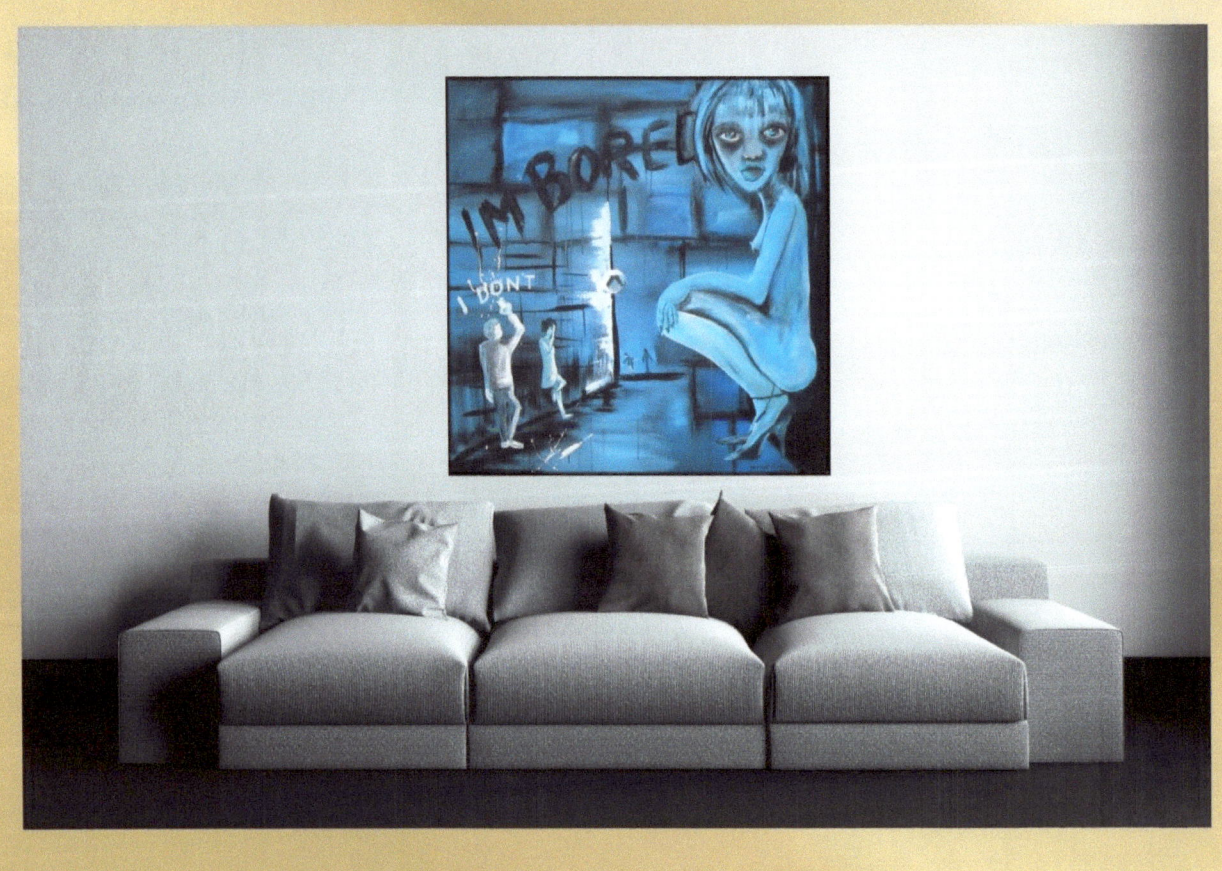

42

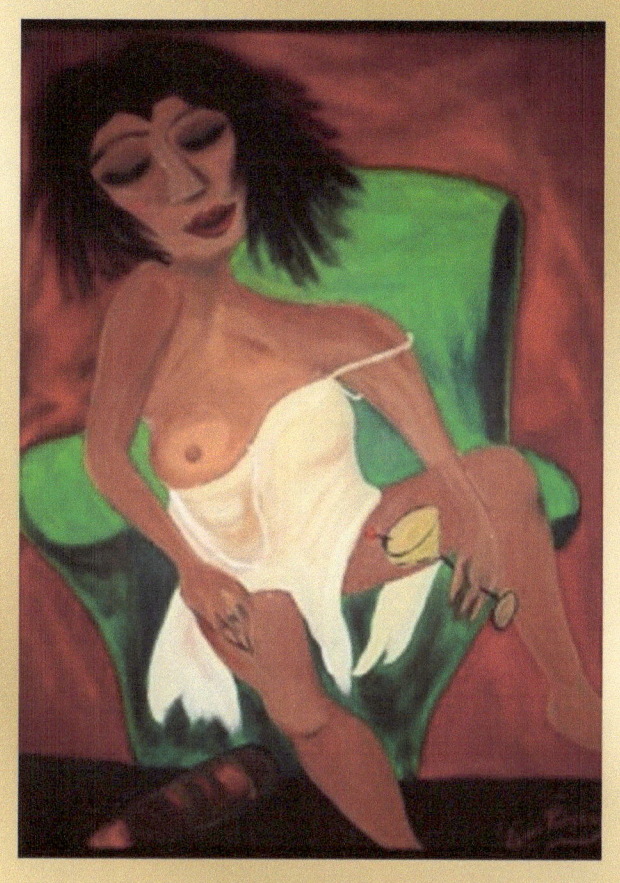

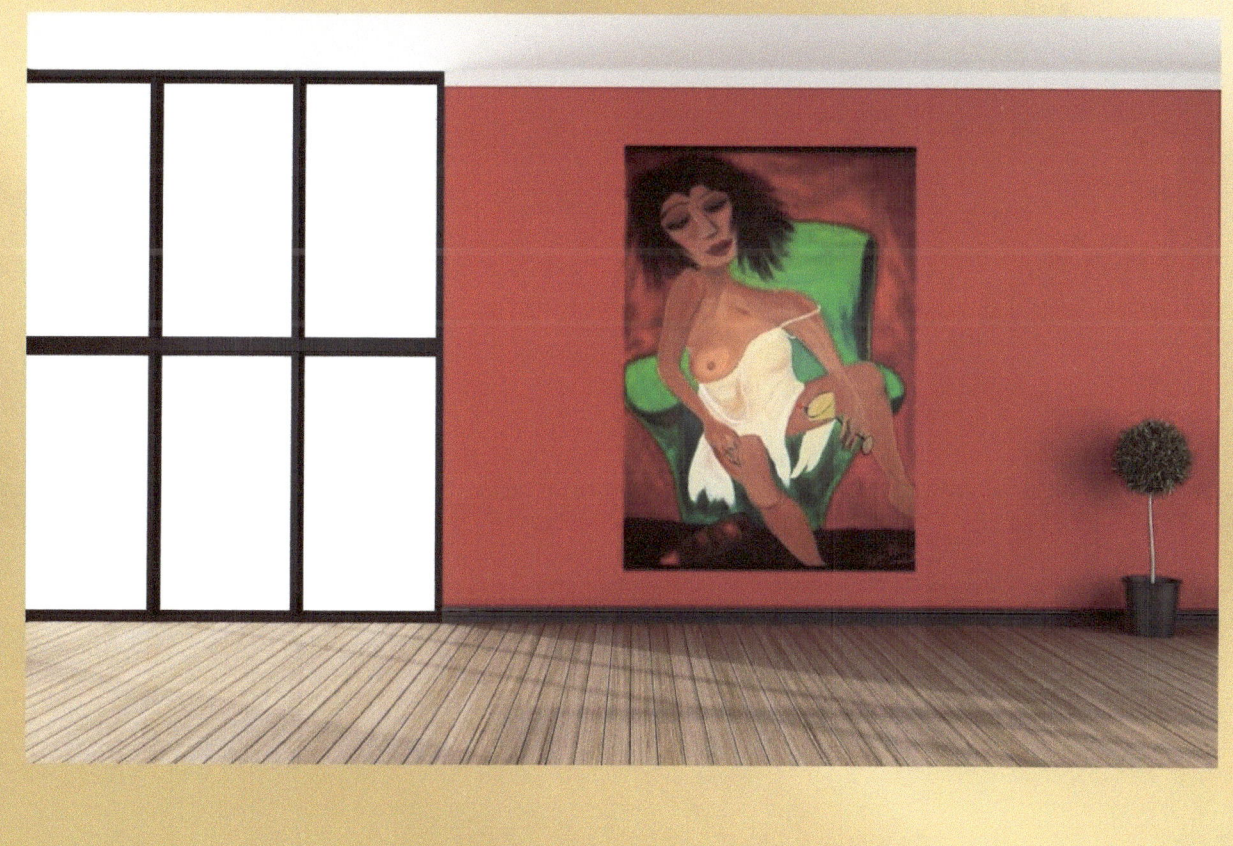